SHIFT:
The Cost of Leadership, The Power of Change

BY CURTIS ADAMS

Copyright © 2025 by Curtis D. Adams

All rights reserved. No part of this book may be reproduced, distributed, or transmitted in any form or by any means, including photocopying, recording, or other electronic or mechanical methods, without the prior written permission of the publisher, except in the case of brief quotations embodied in reviews, critical articles, or educational materials.

DISCLAIMER FOR SHIFT

This book reflects my personal experiences, leadership journey, and research-informed perspectives. The examples and stories are provided for educational and inspirational purposes. They should not be interpreted as legal advice or as the official stance of any organization. References to businesses, leaders, or historical figures are used to highlight leadership principles, and the analysis and interpretations are my own.

IMAGINE A WORLD

WAKE UP INSPIRED

FULFILLED

FEEL SAFE

BELONGING

Curtis Adams

SHIFT: The Cost of Leadership, The Power of Change

I imagine a world where each day begins with inspiration. You rise in the morning not with dread, but with a spark in your heart that reminds you your life matters. Imagine a world where safety is not a privilege, but a promise, where every child, every family, and every worker can breathe without fear. Imagine a world where belonging is the norm, where no one has to question whether they are seen, valued, or loved. And when the day comes to an end, imagine the power of feeling fulfilled, not because the work was easy, but because it mattered.

In this picture, the world is drawn inside of a clock. The clock represents time, the most valuable asset we are given. Every second, every minute, every hour is life ticking forward. As the hands of the clock move, they remind us that inspiration, safety, belonging, and fulfillment are not distant dreams, but choices we must make in the time we have.

This is the world I believe we can build together. A world where waking up inspired, feeling safe, knowing you belong, and ending the day fulfilled are not rare gifts, but everyday realities. That is the bridge we must build, and it begins with valuing time and choosing to live with dignity, courage, and compassion.

SHIFT: The Cost of Leadership, The Power of Change

TABLE OF CONTENTS

DEDICATION **14**
ACKNOWLEDGMENTS **15**
PREFACE **17**
PART ONE: THE FOUNDATION **21**

CHAPTER 1: FROM THE STREETS TO THE BADGE 22
The Monster Dream 22
Choices That Define You 24
Leadership on the Field 25
Leading Without Knowing It 26
College, Mental Health, and Leadership Before Policing 28
The Badge 28
Watch Out 29

CHAPTER 2: CROSSROADS OF TRUST 32
Trust in Mental Health 32
Trust in Juvenile Probation 34
Trust in Policing 35
Authority vs. Trust 36
Watch Out 37

CHAPTER 3: THE WEIGHT OF LEADERSHIP 40
The Weight of Responsibility 41
Lessons from History 42
Lessons from Business 42
The Hidden Cost 43
Watch Out 44

CHAPTER 4: THE COST OF LEADERSHIP 48
The Sacrifice of Time 49
The Modern Burden of the Phone 50
Learning to Let Go 51
The Family Struggle 52

Lessons from History..53
Lessons from Business...53
Watch Out 54

CHAPTER 5: THE ILLUSION OF TITLES 57
Perks and Perceptions 58
Leaders Without Titles..59
A Lesson from History 60
A Lesson from Business..61
Watch Out 61

CHAPTER 6: BUILDING LEADERS, NOT FOLLOWERS... 65
From Followers to Leaders..66
The Right-Hand People 67
The Power of Mentorship and Continuous Learning .. 68
A Lesson from History 69
A Lesson from Business..70
Watch Out 70

CHAPTER 7: BRIDGING GENERATIONS 73
What We Mean by Generations 74
Why Generations Clash 76
Barriers and Truths: What Really Divides Generations 77
Turning Barriers Into Bridges 79
My Own Lessons 80
Watch Out 80
Closing Challenge 82

CHAPTER 8: OVERLOOKED LEADERS: THE POWER OF THE UNSEEN 84
The Nutrition Staff 85
The Custodians 85
The Bus Drivers 86
The Crossing Guards 86
The Nurses and Technicians 87
The Military Sergeants 87
The Administrative and Executive Assistants.............87
The Event and Stadium Staff 88
The Volunteers and Everyday Guides........................88

SHIFT: The Cost of Leadership, The Power of Change

> The Heartbeat of Leadership 89
> Watch Out.. 89
> The Closing Challenge 91

PART TWO: THE CLIMB 93

CHAPTER 9: THE LONELINESS OF COMMAND 94
> The Resistance Within 95
> The Weight of Liability 96
> Drawing from Experience 97
> The Blessing of Support.. 97
> The Loneliness of the Seat..................................... 98
> Building from Scratch 98
> Lessons Beyond Policing.. 98
> Watch Out 99

CHAPTER 10: TRUST EARNED TWICE............ 102
> Trust Beyond Authority 104
> The Accountability Factor..................................... 105
> A Lesson from History 106
> A Lesson from Business 106
> Watch Out... 107

CHAPTER 11: THE GOOD, THE BAD, AND THE UGLY 110
> The Good 111
> The Bad... 111
> The Ugly 112
> A Lesson from History 113
> A Lesson from Business 114
> Watch Out... 114

CHAPTER 12: THE PRICE AND THE PROMISE. 117
> The Economics of Leadership.............................. 118
> The Hidden Cost – Family 118
> The Promise of Change 119
> The Leadership Trade-Off 120
> A Lesson from History 120
> Watch Out... 121

CHAPTER 13: LEADERSHIP WITHOUT BOUNDARIES 125
Leadership in Families.. 125
Leadership in Teams... 126
Leadership in Business and Organizations.............. 127
Leadership in Communities..................................... 127
Lessons Across Boundaries 128
A Lesson from History 128
A Lesson from Business... 129
Watch Out 129

CHAPTER 14: SEEING BEYOND THE HORIZON 132
Casting the Vision 133
Living the Vision 133
Keeping the Vision Alive 134
A Lesson from History 135
A Lesson from Business... 135
Watch Out 135

PART THREE: THE TEST 141

CHAPTER 15: THE CULTURE YOU CREATE 142
Why Culture Matters Everywhere 143
Policing Example: Building Bridges vs. Breaking Trust 144
Lesson for Leaders 144
Business Example: Culture Eats Strategy................ 145
Family Example: Culture at Home 145
Sports Example: Teams That Win and Teams That Rot 146
The Chief's Lens: Lessons from My Own Career 146
A Lesson from History 147
The Turning Point in Policing................................... 147
A Lesson from Business... 148
Watch Out 148

CHAPTER 16: CLIMBING THE LADDER WITHOUT LOSING YOURSELF 151
Level One – Leading Yourself.................................. 152

SHIFT: The Cost of Leadership, The Power of Change

    Level Two – Leading Others 153
    Level Three – Leading Leaders 154
    Level Four – Leading an Organization 155
    Pros and Cons of Moving Up the Ladder 156
    The Survival Tools for All Levels............................. 156
    A Lesson from History 157
    A Lesson from Business 157
    Watch Out 158

CHAPTER 17: LEADING FROM A WHOLE HEART 161
    The Danger of Unresolved Pain 163
    The Power of the Present 163
    Watch Out 163

CHAPTER 18: CARRYING THE LOAD 168
    The Reality of the Load 169
    Why Leaders Must See the Weight 169
    The Currency of Respect 170
    Moving Beyond the Paycheck 171
    What Happens When the Load Is Ignored.............. 171
    What Happens When the Load Is Shared 172
    Leadership Insight 172
    Watch out... 172
    Closing Thought... 174

CHAPTER 19: PURPOSE OVER PAY 176
    The Limits of Compensation.................................. 177
    Why Purpose Matters More Than Pay 177
    The Leader's Responsibility 178
    Guarding Against Exploitation................................ 178
    How Leaders Connect People to Purpose 179
    What Happens When Purpose Is Ignored.............. 179
    What Happens When Purpose Is Elevated............ 180
    Leadership Insight 180
    Watch out... 180
    Closing Thought... 182

CHAPTER 20: THE SILENT EXODUS: WHY GOOD PEOPLE WALK AWAY 183
    Why People Leave Jobs 184

The Family Parallel 185
What My Experience Tells Me 186
The Empty Chair 186
Leadership Response 187
Watch Out 187
The Closing Challenge 189

CHAPTER 21: EXIT SIGNS 190
The Myth: People Only Leave Supervisors 190
Seeing the Real Reasons 191
The Cost of Ignoring Exit Signs 192
How Leaders Can Respond 192
Leadership Insight 193
Watch Out 193
Closing Thought 195

PART FOUR: THE RECKONING 197

CHAPTER 22: THE HAND-ME-DOWN PROBLEM 198
The Cost of Inherited Problems 198
Why It Happens 199
How Leaders Can Respond 200
Leadership Insight 200
Watch Out 201
Closing Thought 202

CHAPTER 23: BEHIND THE SMILE 204
The Flaws of the Interview 205
What Leaders Must Look For 205
Strategies to See Beyond the Smile 206
Why It Matters 207
Leadership Insight 207
Watch Out 207
Closing Thought 209

CHAPTER 24: THEM VERSUS US 210
How the Divide Forms 210
The Cost of Division 211
How Leaders Bridge the Gap 211
Leadership Insight 212

Watch Out 212
Closing Thought 213

CHAPTER 25: DO NOT FORGET WHERE YOU CAME FROM 215
The Danger of Forgetting 216
Why Perspective Matters 216
How Leaders Stay Grounded 217
Leadership Insight 217
Watch Out 217
Closing Thought 219

CHAPTER 26: UNLOCKING DOORS 220
The Danger of Hoarding Knowledge 220
The Truth About Knowledge 221
Two Kinds of Leaders 221
Why Real Leaders Share 222
How to Unlock the Doors 222
Leadership Insight 223
Watch Out 223
Closing Thought 225

CHAPTER 27: ENOUGH IS ENOUGH 226
Why Leaders Hold On Too Long 227
The Cost of Staying Too Long 227
Knowing When to Let Go 228
Lessons from the Street 228
The Baton Test 229
Practical Ways to Finish Well 229
Leadership Insight 229
Watch Out 230
Closing Thought 231

CHAPTER 28: THE SABOTAGE WITHIN 232
Why People Sabotage 233
Who Really Pays the Price 234
The Cost of Sabotage 235
How Leaders Confront Sabotage 236
Watch Out 236
Closing Thought 238

CHAPTER 29: PRESENCE WITHOUT PERFORMANCE **239**
    The Problem Leaders Face 239
    Why It Happens 240
    The Clear Vision Gap 241
    The Hidden Cost of Passion 241
    The Leadership Cost 242
    The Response Leaders Must Take 243
    Watch Out 244
    The Closing Challenge 245

CHAPTER 30: RETIRED ON DUTY **247**
    The Leadership Response 249
    Leadership Insight 249
    Watch Out 250
    Closing Thought 251

CHAPTER 31: THE HIDDEN COST OF ABSENCE **253**
    WATCH OUT 255

CONCLUSION CROSSING THE BRIDGE **258**
    Leadership Snapshot 260

AUTHOR'S NOTE *263*

CALL TO ACTION *265*

ENDNOTES *267*

AUTHOR: CHIEF CURTIS ADAMS *271*

DEDICATION

This book is dedicated to my children and grandchildren. You are my greatest teachers and my greatest reason to keep striving. The lessons I have learned about leadership, sacrifice, and love have been sharpened by being your father and grandfather.

To my children: I know my journey was not always easy for you. There were times I gave more of myself to others than to you. This book is also a bridge back to you, a reminder that I never stopped loving you, and that you were and always will be in my heart.

To my grandchildren: You are the future. I pray that my words and my life's purpose will help build a better path for you. May you grow with courage, humility, and compassion. May you always remember that authentic leadership begins with the act of service.

To my family: Thank you for your patience, your forgiveness, and your love. You have carried me through seasons when the weight of leadership was heavy, and you reminded me of what matters most.

ACKNOWLEDGMENTS

No leader walks alone. This book would not exist without the support, encouragement, and sacrifices of many people along the way.

To the people I have had the privilege to lead: you have taught me as much as I have taught you. Your dedication, your courage, and your willingness to follow the mission have inspired me more than you will ever know.

To my colleagues and mentors in policing, education, and leadership: thank you for challenging me, sharpening me, and holding me accountable. Iron sharpens iron, and I am better because of the wisdom you have shared.

To my friends: you shaped me more than you know. Some of you taught me lessons through the mistakes you made, showing me paths I did not need to take. Others inspired me by the way you rose above the struggles we all faced. Many of us carry scars, but a few of us still walk together, connecting and encouraging one another. To those who are still standing with me today, I am grateful for the bond we built as kids. To those who lost their way, I carry you in my heart as a reminder of why leadership and choices matter.

To the organizations that shaped me: Atlanta Public Schools Police Department, the Atlanta Police Department, Cook County Juvenile Probation, the mental health facilities where I worked early in my career, and the Sheriff's Office in Florida. Each of you gave me lessons, experiences, and opportunities that continue to guide me today. You sharpened my skills, tested my values, and showed me the weight of real leadership.

To the Bibb County School District and the communities I have served: thank you for trusting me with the responsibility to protect, serve, and lead. Your support, your partnership, and your commitment to our shared mission gave me the strength to keep building bridges.

Finally, to all readers of this book: thank you for giving me your time and attention. My hope is that these words do more than inspire you. I hope they remind you that leadership begins at home, and the bridges we build with those closest to us are the ones that endure. I hope that this text will equip you to lead, to change, and to build bridges in your own world.

PREFACE

LEADERSHIP HAS BEEN MY CALLING, as well as my struggle. I did not grow up with a roadmap for success. I grew up in poverty, in neighborhoods where violence and temptation were part of life. I saw friends die. I saw others go to jail. I knew early on that the decisions I made could change the direction of my life.

From the football field to the fraternity house, from mental health centers to juvenile probation, from patrol cars to the Chief's office, my journey has been shaped by one constant truth: leadership matters. Not the kind that hides behind titles or seeks recognition, but the kind that builds trust, makes sacrifices, and creates value for others.

This book is not about being perfect. It is about being real. It is about the cost of leadership, the power of change, and the lessons learned from both triumph and failure. It is about the good, the bad, and the ugly sides of leadership in policing and beyond. It is about choices that save lives and choices that can potentially harm families. It is about balance, sacrifice, accountability, credibility, and hope.

I wrote this book for every leader, whether you wear a badge, carry a briefcase, stand in a classroom, or guide your family at home. Leadership does not belong to titles. It belongs to those who step forward, accept responsibility, and serve.

If you are looking for strategies, you will find some in this book. If you are looking for stories, you will find those too. More than anything, I hope you find yourself in these pages. I hope you see that leadership is not about being the strongest or the smartest. It is about being willing to endure the price so that others can experience the promise of change.

This is more than my story. It is an invitation to cross your own bridge, to embrace the cost, and to discover the leader you were created to be.

SHIFT: The Cost of Leadership, The Power of Change

SHIFT: The Cost of Leadership, The Power of Change

PART ONE:
THE FOUNDATION

The strongest bridges are built on the lessons we learn when no one is watching. My story did not begin in boardrooms or with titles. It began in broken places, where I had to decide who I was going to be. I did not choose the environment into which I was born. I chose how I responded to it and created my own narrative.

The noise, the chaos, the loss... all of it became my classroom. The lessons were not about strategy or management. They were about survival, loyalty, and drawing lines I refused to cross. That is where my leadership began, long before anyone gave me a title. Everything I learned in those early years became the ground I had to stand on. Then it was time to see if it could hold.

CHAPTER 1:
FROM THE STREETS TO THE BADGE

I GREW UP IN A PLACE where struggle was part of life. The streets were alive with noise: the sound of sirens, arguments, laughter, and music integrating. Behind every sound was a story of survival. Opportunities were limited, and danger was close enough to keep you on edge. Within this setting, there were lessons that shaped me.

Trouble was part of the air we breathed. Some of my friends went to jail. Others died before they could experience life. Many fell into drugs, either using or selling. The remaining friends that are still here, we stay connected. We talk, we laugh, we reminisce. Even after everything life threw at us, the bond we built as kids survived. This loyalty taught me something: connection matters more than circumstances.

What set me apart were not the things I did, but the things I refused to do. I refused to smoke marijuana, drink alcohol, or use any other recreational drugs. Even as a child, I knew enough to draw a line. At the time, I thought I was just being stubborn. Now, I understand that those decisions were the first acts of self-leadership. Leadership begins long before anyone gives you a title. You may not face gangs on a corner, but every leader faces crossroads. For some, it is choosing honesty when cutting corners seems easier. For others, it is standing firm when compromise would be more comfortable. Leadership starts with self-discipline, which underpins all other leadership styles.

Before I ever wore a badge, before I ever stood in front of a team, I was leading myself away from destruction. Authentic leadership begins in the dark, shaped by unseen choices that define who you become.

The neighborhood taught me how to read people, how to feel when tension was rising, and how to recognize brokenness and strength. The streets became my first classroom in leadership. They showed me what happens when there is little guidance and what happens when someone has the courage to step forward.

My determination from the start was to walk a different path. The badge did not free me from my past; it gave me purpose. My early years gave me the toughness and the perspective I needed to wear the uniform with purpose. This book begins with the journey from the inner-city streets to the badge. It is not only about where I started, but the shift that happens when hardship is turned into leadership.

THE MONSTER DREAM

I will never forget the dream I had as a young child. My friends had talked about it for weeks. In their dream, a monster swallowed them whole. They could not escape, no matter what they did. Then one night, I had the same dream.

The monster grabbed me, dragging me toward his mouth. I could feel the heat of his breath, the weight of his pull, the darkness waiting to consume me. Most people would have surrendered. Even in that dream, I refused. I reached into his jaws, pulled them apart with my hands, and ripped his head open. His head exploded, and I walked away free.

The next day I told my friends. They laughed. They said it was impossible. I did not argue. Deep down, I knew I was different. Even in my sleep, I chose to fight when others accepted defeat. That was the first time I understood that leadership is not about avoiding the monster. It is about facing it and refusing to be swallowed.

Your monster may not look like mine. It may be fear of failure, the risk of starting a new business, or the pressure of leading a team that doubts you. Every leader encounters something that threatens to consume them. The mark of transformational leadership is choosing courage when surrender feels easier.

CHOICES THAT DEFINE YOU

Growing up in the inner city, choices were constant. Drugs on the corner. Alcohol in the alley. Gangs waiting to recruit at the school gates. Each option looked normal, but each one carried a cost.

One night in an elevator, one of my closest friends decided to rob a man. I told him not to. When the doors opened, the man turned and shot my friend in the groin. He bled out right in front of me. The shooter looked at me, then walked away. I believe I was spared because I chose not to take part. That decision saved my life.

Another time, I watched a friend spin the chamber of a revolver in a game of Russian roulette. He pulled the trigger. The sound echoed in my ears long after the room went silent. He was gone in an instant. I chose not to take part, and that choice saved my life again.

Choices shape life more than circumstances. In the streets, choices that were made meant life or death. In business, they mean trust or betrayal. In families, they mean growth or breakdown. Leadership is the sum of the choices you make when no one else will.

History proves the same. Rosa Parks made one quiet choice to keep her seat on a bus, and a movement was born. Jackie Robinson chose dignity over retaliation, and he changed the face of baseball. Leadership begins not with a title but with a choice that influences others.

LEADERSHIP ON THE FIELD

Sports became the stage where my choices turned into influence. My first year of high school, my brother died. I could have quit. Instead, I threw myself into football because that was how he remembered me.

I always tried to work harder than anyone else. I stayed after practice, doing extra workouts. I pushed my coach's car around the parking lot to build strength. I was not the most talented, but effort has its own power. It earned me respect, and respect earned me the leadership role as captain.

By the time I graduated from high school, I became captain of both the football and wrestling teams. I was recognized as a Blue Chip All-American, recruited by Division One and Big Ten schools, and earned a scholarship to Northern Illinois University. I was also the first athlete at my high school to pass the ACT standardized test to be eligible to play college football. Something people thought could not be done. That moment was bigger than a test. It was leadership, showing others what was possible when you commit yourself.

The greatest leaders are not always the most gifted. They are the ones who give relentless effort when others quit. That commitment inspires trust and earns respect. This is the essence of authentic leadership, where character and consistency outweigh talent or titles.

LEADING WITHOUT KNOWING IT

Looking back, I realized I was already practicing leadership without knowing it. I did not have a title. I did not see myself as a leader. Teammates followed my example. Friends listened when I spoke. My determination gave others courage.

Leadership does not start with authority. It starts with influence. A teenager who resists peer pressure is leading. An employee who sets a standard of excellence without a promotion is leading. A parent who models integrity is leading. You do not need a badge to be a leader. You need courage and consistency.

COLLEGE, MENTAL HEALTH, AND LEADERSHIP BEFORE POLICING

My leadership journey continued in college, where I joined a fraternity that became both a brotherhood and a training ground. I was chosen to represent my chapter at national conventions, a responsibility that taught me how to carry the voice of many while standing in front of leaders from across the country. Those experiences sharpened my ability to communicate, build consensus, and carry myself with confidence in unfamiliar spaces. It was in those rooms that I learned leadership is not about being the loudest voice, but about being the steady one that others can depend on.

My first job out of college, I worked in mental health. I cared for children in crisis. Some were placed in padded rooms when their emotions took over. My role was not to punish them. I helped them calm down by sitting with them. I reminded them that they were still human. That required patience and compassion of servant leadership, before I knew the term.

Later, I worked with adults in transition. I taught life skills such as cooking, cleaning, budgeting, and more. These were not small tasks. They restored dignity. I realized leadership was not about giving orders. It was about giving people tools to live.

As a juvenile probation officer, I mentored kids who looked like me. Kids who stood at the same crossroads I once faced. They were one decision away from jail, drugs, or death. My job was not just to enforce conditions. It was to show them a different path. Again, transformational leadership, inspiring others by example.

Those roles prepared me for policing in ways no academy ever could. They taught me that leadership means believing in people when they do not believe in themselves.

THE BADGE

When I joined the Atlanta Police Department, I thought the badge itself would command respect. I quickly learned that it gave me authority but not trust. Authority is given. Trust is earned.

Communities did not respect uniforms unless the person inside it respected them first. I saw officers cross lines that were forbidden. I saw people hurt who should have been protected and helped. I decided I would not lead that way. I would not let a badge become a weapon.

Instead, I chose to lead with restraint, respect, and responsibility. That choice earned me trust; something no rank or title could ever guarantee. That trust became the foundation of leadership lessons I carried into the Chief's role years later.

SHIFT: The Cost of Leadership, The Power of Change

WATCH OUT

Do not confuse authority with leadership. Authority is given. Leadership is earned.

PLAIN INSIGHT

Leadership begins long before the title. It begins with the choices you make when no one is watching.

CASE STUDY: THE YOUNG CAPTAIN

Think of a young captain on a team. Not the most talented nor boisterous person, but the one who works harder than anyone else. That is the person teammates listen to. That is leadership.

TOOL: THE LEADERSHIP TIMELINE

Mark five moments where you led without a title. Write what each moment taught you.

DRILL: LEAD YOURSELF FIRST

For the next week, pick one area to discipline yourself: waking up earlier, eating healthier, or being more present with your family. Track your progress. Leadership begins with self-control.

REFLECTION QUESTIONS

1. What was your first leadership experience?
2. Who trusted you before you had authority?
3. How did your childhood shape your definition of leadership?
4. When did you have to lead yourself through unfairness?
5. What choices are you making now that define your future?

MODERN CONNECTION

Leadership still begins without titles. Children lead their peers. Employees without management roles shape their company's culture. Parents lead their homes. Leadership is everywhere, and those who accept it early shape the world.

LEADERSHIP BRIDGE

I am not a leader because of a badge. I am a leader because of the choices I made before I wore one.

CHAPTER 2:
CROSSROADS OF TRUST

TRUST IS LEADERSHIP'S TRUE CURRENCY. Without it, authority is only a title. With it, leadership becomes influence that outlasts positions and jobs. Authority can be given in a moment, but trust must be earned over time.

In each job I held before law enforcement, trust decided whether people followed me or resisted me. It was never about how loud my voice was or what rules I enforced. It was about whether people trusted me and believed I cared.

TRUST IN MENTAL HEALTH

When I worked in mental health, I quickly discovered that I could not simply walk into a room and say, "I understand you." The people I worked with were living through schizophrenia, depression, and bipolar disorder. They were not naïve. They saw through empty words and hollow gestures. Struggle did not rob them of intelligence or discernment.

If a child told me they were hearing voices, I could not respond with, "Yes, I know," and expect them to trust me. That would have been insulting. Instead, I had to listen with patience. I had to sit down, make eye contact, and remain consistent. I had to prove that I cared about their reality, not about finishing my shift or checking a box on a form. Over time, the only bridge that allowed me to help them was trust.

No leader can demand trust. Whether you are a teacher, CEO, coach, or parent, people measure you by your patience, honesty, and consistency. Servant leadership thrives here, because influence grows when people know you will put their needs before your own.

This is also the discipline of authentic leadership. Trust is built by aligning words and actions, by choosing honesty even when the truth is inconvenient, and by being reliable in both small and large matters. The moment you stop proving yourself is the moment trust begins to erode.

This is not just true in mental health. It is true in families where children test whether their parents really hear them. It is true in schools where students know which teachers genuinely care. It is true in businesses where employees measure leaders by consistency more than charisma. Across all fields, trust is not given out of obligation. It is earned through honesty and consistency. That is authentic leadership in its simplest form.

TRUST IN JUVENILE PROBATION

When I became a juvenile probation officer in Cook County, the importance of trust grew even clearer. My caseload was filled with children society had written off. Judges saw them as numbers. Teachers lost hope. Even their families had given up in most cases. Many of the kids came from backgrounds like mine. They spoke the same language of survival that I had cultivated.

I built trust the only way I knew how: by showing up, listening, and by telling the truth without judgment. They tested me every day. They wanted to know if I would desert them the way others had. I stayed. I did not sugarcoat their mistakes. I never abandoned them in their struggles. That consistency became proof that I was different.

You may never work with children in crisis, but you will lead people who have been overlooked or doubted. Every leader must choose whether to see people as a burden or as potential. Trust is earned when you stay long enough to prove that your words and actions align.

I will never forget when the *Chicago Times* ran a two-page article about me and my work with juveniles. One of the kids I supervised told the reporter, "Mr. Adams was an answer to my prayers." That statement was not about probation rules or conditions. It was not about authority. It was about trust. He believed me when I told him I cared, and that trust gave me the ability to guide him towards change.

That was servant leadership in action: putting someone else's needs first, even when it was inconvenient, when it cost more of my time, and when it required patience that challenged me. Trust turned the relationship from enforcement into influence.

TRUST IN POLICING

When I entered policing, trust became the biggest challenge of all. I was assigned to some of the toughest neighborhoods in Atlanta, then later in Florida. The first thing I learned was that no one trusted me. Not the kids. Not the parents. Not the business owners.

Children ran from police cars as if it were a sport. Parents told their children not to talk to the police. I remember walking down blocks where doors shut at the sight of a uniform. I carried authority but not trust.

I applied what I learned in mental health and probation. I listened. I was consistent. I told the truth, even when it was uncomfortable. I treated people with respect, even when they were disrespectful towards me. Slowly, things began to change.

By the time I left those communities, parents who once told their children to avoid me were calling me directly. Families who feared police officers gave me their phone numbers. Some trusted me enough to bring their kids to me when they had outstanding warrants, because they trusted that I would handle the situation with fairness and dignity. That kind of trust cannot be given by wearing a badge. It must be earned by character.

Authority can make people comply, but it cannot make them believe. Trust turns obedience into commitment and presence into loyalty. This is the enduring trait of credible leadership, where character is the foundation that holds influence together. It was transformational leadership at work: not just changing the way people saw me but changing the way they saw policing itself.

AUTHORITY VS. TRUST

Authority can be given with a badge, a title, or a position. Authority without trust will usually fail. People may comply with authority, but they will not follow it with their commitment.

Trust is different. It cannot be handed down in a promotion or a ceremony. It is earned in the small moments, being consistent when no one is watching, listening when it would be easier to talk, telling the truth even when it's uncomfortable, and at a cost.

A manager can require an employee to show up on time. A parent can demand respect from a child. A chief can require officers to follow procedures. Yet, none of those guarantees trust. Trust comes only when people believe that you mean what you say, and that you will stand by them when it matters the most.

As a leader, you must constantly ask yourself: Am I leaning on authority, or am I building trust? One lasts as long as your title. The other lasts as long as your character.

WATCH OUT

Do not mistake authority for influence. You can force compliance, but you cannot force trust.

PLAIN INSIGHT

Trust is earned in drops and lost in buckets.

CASE STUDY: GAINING TRUST

A new supervisor tried to fix morale with rules. Nothing changed. She switched to weekly listening circles and followed through on small promises. Turnover dropped. Rules did not move people. Trust did.

TOOL: THE TRUST TEST

Ask yourself three questions:

1. Am I consistent in my actions and words?
2. Do people believe I am honest, even when I tell them hard truths?
3. Do I listen more than I speak?

If the answer is yes to all three, you are building trust. If the answer is no to any of them, trust will typically be fragile, no matter what title you hold.

DRILL: PRACTICE LISTENING

Spend one full day focusing on listening. When someone speaks to you, whether it is a family member, coworker, or stranger, do not interrupt. Repeat back what they said in your own words to show that you were listening. Listening is one of the fastest ways to build trust.

REFLECTION QUESTIONS

1. Who trusted you when you had no authority?
2. Who respects your position but does not yet trust you as a person?
3. What actions do you take consistently that prove reliability?
4. How do you respond when trust is broken?
5. In your life today, do you lead more with authority or with trust?

MODERN CONNECTION

In today's world, trust is a valuable asset in leadership. Employees will leave jobs when trust is broken, even if the pay is good. Children will rebel against parents they do not trust, even if rules are strict. Communities will resist leaders they do not trust, even if those leaders carry power.

From the boardroom to the classroom, from the church to the patrol car, trust is the bridge that connects authority to influence. Without it, leadership collapses. With it, leadership creates change that lasts for generations.

LEADERSHIP BRIDGE

I am not followed because of my authority. I am followed because of the trust I build through honesty, consistency, and listening.

CHAPTER 3:
THE WEIGHT OF LEADERSHIP

I QUICKLY LEARNED THAT LEADERSHIP can be a lonely road. The badge gave me authority, but it did not give me acceptance. In many cases, it created distance. Some saw me as a symbol of protection. Others saw me as an enemy. The badge was heavy not because of the metal itself, but because of the expectations and feelings it carried.

Inside the department, I saw officers misuse their authority, crossing lines that left scars on communities that were already hurting. I knew then that leadership was not only about dealing with criminals or enforcing laws. At times, it meant standing up to your own peers.

I will never forget the night we were chasing a suspect. I caught him and had him under control, ready to place the cuffs. Another officer ran up behind me with a baton raised. The suspect was subdued, yet the officer prepared to strike. I stopped him. In that moment, leadership meant risking the criticism of my own colleagues to do what was right.

That choice did not win me any friends in the office. Some saw me as weak for not "backing the blue" in the way they defined it. However, in the eyes of the community, that moment fostered trust. Parents who once shut their doors when patrol cars rolled by started opening them when they saw me. People noticed that I refused to let authority turn into abuse. Leadership is not conforming to the culture around you, but holding the line when others look away.

Leadership will often cost you popularity. It may isolate you in a boardroom, on a campus, or even within your own circle of friends. But ethical leadership is measured not by how many agree with you, but by whether you have the courage to act with integrity when no one else will.

THE WEIGHT OF RESPONSIBILITY

The pressure of leadership in policing is unlike most professions. In many jobs, a mistake can cost money or taint your reputation. In policing, a mistake can cost a life. You carry a firearm and the legal authority to take away someone's freedom. Decisions are scrutinized, not only by your supervisors, but also by the people you serve, and perhaps the entire nation. That weight is relentless.

There were nights I lay awake wondering if I had made the right call. Did I de-escalate fast enough? Did I use too much force? Did I let someone go who might hurt someone else? Leadership in law enforcement means living with decisions that echo in your mind long after the shift ends.

The weight is not always bad. It can strengthen you if you learn how to carry it. Conflict, decisions, and confrontation became another weight that built my endurance. The pressure forced me to grow. Leadership is not about escaping responsibility. It is about learning how to carry it without being crushed.

LESSONS FROM HISTORY

This tension between authority and responsibility is not unique to policing. History is filled with leaders who carried the weight of responsibility when it would have been easier to quit.

Consider Abraham Lincoln during the Civil War. The nation was torn apart. He was mocked, underestimated, and even hated by many. Yet he carried the responsibility for unity and freedom on his shoulders. Lincoln understood that "character is like a tree and reputation like a shadow. The shadow is what we think of it; the tree is the real thing." He knew that authority without integrity could destroy a nation. His test was greater than mine, but the principle was the same: authority without trust leads to collapse.

LESSONS FROM BUSINESS

Leadership lessons also come from the corporate world. Howard Schultz, the former CEO of Starbucks, stepped back into his company when it was failing. He did not return with a stack of orders. He returned with humility. He visited stores, sat with employees, asked questions, and listened. By showing honesty and consistency, he rebuilt trust and restored the brand.

The setting was different, but the weight was the same: responsibility over authority. Schultz proved that listening can be more powerful than commanding, and that trust outlasts titles.

The same principle applies in classrooms, churches, nonprofits, and families. Leadership should never be about perks or titles. It is about responsibility. Titles are fragile. Trust is lasting.

THE HIDDEN COST

There is also a personal cost to leadership that few people understand. When you carry the weight of responsibility, it does not leave when you clock out. It follows you home. It affects your sleep, your patience, and sometimes your family. Leaders often spend more time serving others than serving their own households. That imbalance is a hidden cost that leaders must acknowledge.

I have missed family events, holidays, and birthdays because of the responsibilities I carried. Those moments taught me that the weight of leadership must be balanced with the weight of family. Leadership is not only about carrying responsibility at work. It is about ensuring that responsibility does not crush the relationships that matter the most.

Many leaders feel this weight. Executives sacrifice dinners at home. Teachers sacrifice weekends. Parents sacrifice rest for the sake of their children. The key trait is balance, because leadership that wins outside but fails at home leaves scars that no applause can cover.

WATCH OUT

Do not confuse popularity with leadership. Leadership often requires you to stand alone.

PLAIN INSIGHT

Responsibility is heavy, but the weight of doing what is right strengthens you more than it burdens you.

CASE STUDY: THE BATON INCIDENT

That night when I stopped a fellow officer from striking a suspect who was already under control, I did not gain popularity. In fact, it made me a target for whispers and side comments. However, I received something greater. I earned trust from the community. They saw that not all officers looked the other way. That trust lasted longer than the awkward stares in the locker room. Authority grants power, but trust decides if your actions endure.

TOOL: THE RESPONSIBILITY GAUGE

Ask yourself three questions when facing a tough decision:

1. Am I choosing what is easiest or what is right?
2. Am I protecting my reputation or protecting people?
3. If no one supported me, would I still make this choice?

Your honest answers will reveal whether you are carrying leadership with integrity or hiding behind authority.

DRILL: PRACTICE INTEGRITY IN SMALL THINGS

For one week, focus on the smallest choices. Keep the promises you make, even the ones that seem insignificant. Do not cut corners. Do not tell half-truths. Integrity in small things builds the strength to carry greater responsibilities.

REFLECTION QUESTIONS

1. When have you stood alone for what was right?
2. Have you ever confused popularity with leadership?
3. How do you respond to the weight of responsibility in your life?
4. What choices today are preparing you for bigger challenges tomorrow?
5. What does integrity mean to you in your field of work?

MODERN CONNECTION

In today's culture, leadership is often confused with fame. Social media celebrates likes, followers, and attention, but leadership is not about applause. It is about accountability. The true test of leadership is not how many people cheer for you, but how many trust you when no one is watching.

A supervisor in a warehouse, a coach on a high school team, a mother raising children, a CEO leading a company, all of them carry a weight that is not glamorous but is essential. The weight of leadership is heavy because it requires sacrifice. That sacrifice is what separates real leaders from pretenders.

> **LEADERSHIP BRIDGE**
> I do not lead because I am popular. I lead because I am willing to carry the weight of responsibility, even when it means standing alone.

CHAPTER 4:
THE COST OF LEADERSHIP

I THOUGHT THE LEADERSHIP TITLES would bring more support. I thought stepping into the role of leadership meant I would have more people standing with me, guiding me, and helping me carry the weight. Instead, I found myself standing in some of the loneliest places of my career. The badge gave me authority, but the responsibility it carried came with a cost.

What I learned quickly was that leadership often required sacrifices most people will never see. The public sees the uniform, the title, and the authority. They do not see the long hours that rob you of family moments, the stress that seeps into relationships, or the decisions that haunt you long after you hang up the uniform. Leadership does not just require your time. It drains energy, peace of mind, and even your health.

THE SACRIFICE OF TIME

The first impact I felt most deeply was time. I cannot count the number of nights when my phone rang after midnight with a call that could not wait until morning. Crises did not care that my children had games or that my family was gathered for dinner. Reports, investigations, and emergencies demanded attention at the exact moment when my family needed me most.

Leaders understand this sacrifice in their own way. Parents sacrifice sleep to care for a newborn. Entrepreneurs work late into the night trying to keep a business alive. Teachers spend weekends grading papers and preparing lessons. Pastors spend holidays visiting families in hospitals while their own families celebrate without them. The cost of time is not unique to police. It is the universal price of leadership.

Time is one of our most valuable assets. Money can be gained and lost. Titles can be given and taken away. Once time is spent, it cannot be regained. For years, I gave nearly all of my time to the badge. At first, I told myself I was doing it for my family, to provide and protect. Eventually, I realized that if I were not careful, leadership would leave the people closest to me feeling forgotten.

That realization made me see that leaders must count the cost. Sacrifice is part of leadership. But if you sacrifice everything, you risk losing the very people you claim to love.

THE MODERN BURDEN OF THE PHONE

One of the hardest lessons learned was how to manage the constant demand of the phone. It was constantly on my desk, in my car, or by my bed. It became my alarm clock, my late-night knock at the door, and my reminder that leadership does not sleep.

There is a difference between resting and waiting. When you keep a phone by your head, you are not truly resting. You are waiting for the next call, waiting for the next crisis, waiting for the next piece of news that might turn a quiet night into chaos. That kind of constant availability is one of the most exhausting realities of modern leadership.

Balance came only by building a trusted team. No leader carries the burden alone. You need go-to people. People you can count on to carry the weight when you cannot. Leadership will always fall back on your shoulders. When you have dependable people standing beside you, the load becomes lighter.

This is why building leaders under you is not optional. It is essential. If you are the only one holding the mission together, the mission will collapse the moment you step away.

LEARNING TO LET GO

Another hidden cost of leadership is letting go of the job you once loved. Most leaders, especially in policing, struggle with this. Officers rise through the ranks by proving their skill, their courage, and their ability to do the job under pressure. When they become supervisors, they carry the mindset that no one can do the job better than they can. I felt that same pull.

Leadership is not about holding on to the old job. It is about stepping into a new one. The work that used to be mine was no longer my responsibility. My new responsibility was to manage the people doing the work, to guide their personalities, navigate their conflicts, and help them succeed in their own roles. It also meant accepting that their way of doing things might not look like mine, and that was not a failure; it was growth.

One of the greatest mistakes leaders make is refusing to delegate. They hold on so tightly that they burn themselves out. Worse, they rob others of the opportunity to rise.

Growth demands release. Leaders who refuse to delegate may achieve short-term results, but they will never build long-term sustainability. This is empowering leadership, marked by the ability to multiply strength in others rather than hoard it for yourself.

THE FAMILY STRUGGLE

Perhaps the hardest cost of all is the toll on family. For years, my family received what was left of me after the job. My community, my officers, and the mission consumed the best of my energy. My children often felt my absence. My family sacrificed for the badge even though they never wore it.

This is not unique to me. Leaders in all professions face this struggle. Business executives miss family dinners. Teachers give their evenings to students instead of spouses. Coaches spend weekdays and weekends on the road while their children grow up at home in their absence. For some it is the business trip that takes them away. For others, it is the constant phone call that interrupts family time. This is where the trait of empathy becomes critical. Leaders must recognize that the cost is not theirs alone. Those who love them often pay the same price. Leadership can inspire many, but if it leaves your family feeling abandoned, the success is insufficient.

I realized that leadership is not only about building others up. It is about protecting the foundation of your own home. If the people who love you most cannot trust your leadership, no title, no applause, and no recognition will ever fill that void.

LESSONS FROM HISTORY

WINSTON CHURCHILL: STEADFAST IN CRISIS

During World War II, Britain faced daily bombings, fear, and the possibility of invasion. Churchill's speeches gave people courage when defeat seemed inevitable. His ability to speak honestly about danger while still inspiring hope kept a nation united through its darkest hours.

Lesson: Leaders steady the hearts of others when fear threatens to tear them apart. His story is a reminder that the struggle between mission and family is not new. Leaders must wrestle with how to balance both, knowing that neither can be ignored without consequence.

LESSONS FROM BUSINESS

The same truth is in corporate leadership. Indra Nooyi, former CEO of PepsiCo, once shared how she felt torn between boardroom responsibilities and family responsibilities. She admitted the guilt of missing milestones at home even as she guided one of the largest corporations in the world. She spoke honestly about the reality that leaders cannot "have it all." Something usually gives.

Her words echo what many leaders feel, though rarely say aloud: leadership requires sacrifice. Balance is not something you find once, but something you fight for daily.

WATCH OUT

Leadership will take as much from you as you allow. If you do not protect your time and your family, the cost will be greater than the reward.

PLAIN INSIGHT

Leadership is never free. The price is time, energy, and relationships. The return is measured in lives changed and legacies built.

CASE STUDY: BALANCING THE BADGE

I had to learn to create space for my family while carrying the weight of a department. There were times when I failed at that balance. Failure taught me as much as success. Leadership without balance leaves scars that no title can cover. The true test of leadership is not only what you build in your organization, but what you protect inside your own home.

TOOL: THE BALANCE CHECK

Ask yourself weekly:

1. Did I give my family my best attention this week?
2. Did I give my health the care it needed?
3. Did I give my team the direction they deserved?

If the answer is no to any of these, your leadership is out of balance.

DRILL: PROTECT YOUR TIME

For one week, set aside a non-negotiable block of time for family or personal renewal. Guard it as fiercely as you would a critical meeting at work. Time is leadership's most valuable resource, and protecting it is an act of discipline as well as love.

REFLECTION QUESTIONS

1. What sacrifices have you made in your leadership journey?
2. Which of those sacrifices were worth it, and which were not?
3. How do you measure the balance between your mission and your family?

4. Who in your life has felt the cost of your leadership the most?
5. How will you protect your time moving forward?

MODERN CONNECTION

In today's world, leaders are tempted to chase productivity, profit, and recognition as if they are the true signs of success. However, none of those things can replace time. Money can be earned, lost, and regained. Recognition can fade. Titles can be stripped away. However, once time is gone, it is gone forever.

That is why the best leaders measure success not only in what they build outside but also in what they preserve inside. They know that true wealth is not stored in bank accounts, but in memories. True influence is not measured in applause, but in the people who know you best and still believe in you.

LEADERSHIP BRIDGE

I am willing to pay the cost of leadership, but I refuse to let that cost take away what matters most.

CHAPTER 5:
THE ILLUSION OF TITLES

ONE OF THE HARDEST TRUTHS about leadership is realizing that titles do not make you a leader. Titles give you authority, but authority is different from influence. I have seen people with rank, stripes, or fancy corporate titles who could not inspire anyone to follow them once the title was gone.

The test of leadership is simple: if you strip away the title, will anyone follow you? If the answer is no, then you were never truly leading. You were only occupying a position. This question belongs to every field. Remove CEO, superintendent, pastor, or chief, and the truth remains. Do people follow you for who you are, or only because of what you represent? Titles fade, but strong character is what keeps people walking beside you when the title is gone.

I worked alongside officers who had no rank, yet commanded respect when they spoke. They did not need a stripe on their sleeve. Their honesty and courage spoke louder than any symbol of authority. In contrast, I saw supervisors whose stripes gave them compliance but not trust. The moment they walked out of the room, their influence disappeared.

That difference taught me a lesson I carry with me to this day: positions can be taken away in an instant, but character cannot.

PERKS AND PERCEPTIONS

Titles often come with perks. People open doors for you. They stand when you walk into the room. They listen more carefully to your words. They smile when you pass them in the hallway. Many of those actions are not about who you are. They are about what you stand for.

Remove the title, and many of those benefits vanish. The reserved parking spot is no longer yours. The special invitations stop coming. The flattering words become less frequent. If you mistake those perks for respect, you will eventually be crushed when they disappear.

Respect comes from character, consistency, and service, not by the title printed on a nameplate. Titles are temporary. Character is lasting.

LEADERS WITHOUT TITLES

Some of the best leaders I have ever seen never had official titles. I saw it on the football field growing up. There was typically a kid who worked harder than anyone else, who encouraged teammates, and led by example. Coaches may have named someone else captain, but everyone knew who the real leader was.

I have seen employees in offices who were not managers influence the culture more than their bosses. They did it through their consistency, their positivity, and their willingness to help others. I have seen community members lead movements without ever being elected or appointed. Leadership without a title is often the purest form of influence because it is earned, not assigned.

Those experiences remind us that leadership is not about authority. It is about influence. Authority can make people comply. Influence inspires people to follow.

For many leaders, titles become a trap, especially for those who were particularly good at their jobs before being promoted. They cannot let go of the work they used to do. They believe no one can do the job better than they can. As a result, they hover, micromanage, and refuse to delegate.

That mindset burns leaders out. It also stunts the growth of their people. When you accept a leadership role, your job is no longer to prove how good you are at the old job. Your job is to develop and guide the people who do the work. That shift takes humility to step back, patience to teach, and wisdom to let others succeed in their own way.

I had to learn this lesson the hard way. There were times when I thought, "If I just take over, I know it will get done right." Every time I gave into that mindset, I robbed someone else of their chance at growth. Leadership is not about holding on. It is about letting go so that others can rise.

A LESSON FROM HISTORY

History has often rewarded those who understand that leadership is greater than titles. During the Revolutionary War, George Washington was one of the clearest examples. After leading the Continental Army to victory, he could have taken power for himself. The people were ready to make him a king. Instead, he stepped down and returned to private life.

Washington's decision shocked the world. Monarchs in Europe could not understand it. This set the tone for what American leadership should look like: service over self, influence over position. Washington proved that leadership was not about clinging to power. It was about leaving a legacy greater than his own ambition.

A LESSON FROM BUSINESS

Jim Collins, in his research for the book *Good to Great*, described "Level 5 Leaders." These leaders built lasting organizations not through charisma or titles but through humility, discipline, and the ability to empower others. Their companies thrived long after they stepped down because their leadership was never about them.

That is the mark of a true leader: when the work continues even after you are gone. Titles pass from one person to another. Influence outlives them all.

WATCH OUT

Titles are temporary. Influence lasts. Do not let your worth be tied to a position.

PLAIN INSIGHT

If no one will follow you without the title, you are not leading. You are only occupying a seat.

CASE STUDY: LEADERSHIP WITHOUT STRIPES

I worked alongside officers who had no rank yet led more effectively than their supervisors. They did not have authority, but their teammates respected them because of their work ethic, their honesty, and their consistency. When they spoke, people listened. When they acted, others followed. That is leadership without a title. It is often more powerful than rank. This is authentic leadership at its core. Influence without a title is the purest kind because it cannot be forced. It is earned through work ethic, consistency, and trust. Leadership rooted in authenticity will always outlast leadership rooted in authority.

TOOL: THE TITLE TEST

Ask yourself:

1. If I lost my title today, who would still follow me?
2. Am I leaning on my position, or am I building trust?
3. Do people respect me for who I am, or only for what I represent?

DRILL: LEAD WITHOUT LABELS

For one week, avoid using your title in discussions. Lead by action, listening, and influence. Pay attention to who responds to you and why.

REFLECTION QUESTIONS

1. What perks come with your title?
2. If your title were taken away tomorrow, would people still trust and follow you?
3. How have you seen people lead without official titles?
4. Are you empowering others to lead, or holding onto control?
5. How does your character speak louder than your position?

MODERN CONNECTION

In today's world, titles are glorified. CEO, CFO, Director, Chief. They sound impressive, but without substance they are hollow. Employees do not stay in jobs because of fancy titles. They stay because of leaders they trust. Communities do not respect leaders for their positions. They respect them for their character. Children do not follow parents because of their role. They follow them because of love and consistency.

Leadership is not about what you are called. It is about who you are when the title is gone.

> **LEADERSHIP BRIDGE**
> A title may open doors, but only character keeps them open.

CHAPTER 6:
BUILDING LEADERS, NOT FOLLOWERS

ONE OF THE GREATEST RESPONSIBILITIES of leadership is multiplying yourself in others. True leaders do not measure success by the number of people who fall in line behind them. They measure it by the number of people who rise because of them. Authority may bring compliance, yet only trust and influence inspire people to grow into leaders themselves.

When I first stepped into leadership, I believed it was enough to be respected for what I knew and how hard I worked. Over time, I realized that real leadership is not about being the most skilled or the strongest in the room. It is about creating an environment where others discover their own strength. My job was no longer to prove myself. My job was to unlock the potential in others.

That shift requires patience when mistakes are made, humility to step back, and courage to allow others to take the lead even when you know you could do it faster yourself. The reward comes when those who look to you for every answer begin making decisions, taking ownership, and guiding others. That is when you know you are building leaders.

Many leaders struggle with this lesson because they believe no one can do the job as well as they can. If everything depends on you, you have not led. You have only managed. Leadership is not about control. It is about releasing control so others can rise.

FROM FOLLOWERS TO LEADERS

Leadership is not measured by followers, but by leaders you build. If the organization only functions when you are present, then you have failed as a leader.

This is one of the most important lessons I learned in my early supervisory roles. I knew that if I wanted to prepare for higher responsibility, I could not be the one doing everything. I had to prepare others to carry the mission.

That understanding shaped how I approached leadership when I became Chief. I was ready to make immediate changes. I knew what to look for in people. I knew which values mattered most and how to align the department with a bigger plan. I promoted and trained people not just to fill positions, but to embody the mission and values of the department.

I reminded them consistently: the mission is why we exist, and the vision is where we are going. If we do not know where we are going, then any road will get us there. Leaders must make sure the path is clear and that the team is walking in the same direction.

THE RIGHT-HAND PEOPLE

A leader cannot do it all alone. Great leaders have right-hand people, trusted men and women who carry the mission when the leader cannot be everywhere at once.

I built my team carefully, choosing people not because of politics or popularity, but because of shared values. When I gave them responsibility, I gave them freedom too. They did not have to do the job the way I would have done it. They simply had to get the job done with integrity and commitment to the mission.

That trust freed me from the burden of micromanaging and freed them to grow into leaders themselves. The strongest organizations do not rise or fall on one person. They succeed because of the depth of leadership across the ranks. The mission is never safe in the hands of one. It is only secure when it rests in the hands of many. Transformational leaders understand this truth. They multiply themselves by building other leaders. The trait of humility makes this possible because it requires releasing control so others can rise.

This is succession. Leadership is not just about what you accomplish while you wear the title. It is about whether the work continues when you are gone.

THE POWER OF MENTORSHIP AND CONTINUOUS LEARNING

Another key to making this transition is having mentors and role models who can guide you through it. No leader grows in isolation. I have been shaped by people who were willing to tell me the truth, encourage me when I doubted myself, and challenge me when I became too comfortable.

That is why mentorship is critical. Leaders need others they can look to for wisdom, perspective, and accountability. A mentor helps you see the bigger picture when all you can see is the daily grind.

The other key is continuous training. Leadership is not something you learn once and then master forever. It is something you must continually sharpen.

Organizations like FBI-LEEDA, the International Association of Chiefs of Police, and national leadership conferences provide opportunities to keep sharpening your law enforcement skills. Local and state programs also offer tools to adapt to changing times.

The moment a leader stops learning is the moment they stop growing. Leaders who do not invest in their own development cannot expect to develop others. That is why it is critical to seek training, embrace mentorship, and remain a student no matter how high your title is. Leadership is a life-long apprenticeship. The trait of curiosity keeps leaders sharp, while the style of continuous learning keeps organizations alive. The best leaders are students first, and it is their humility that allows them to raise others to stand even taller.

A LESSON FROM HISTORY

General Dwight Eisenhower, who later became President, was known for his ability to delegate. During World War II, he commanded the largest allied force in history. He could not be everywhere at once, so he built a team of strong commanders. He trusted them with authority and decision-making, even when he disagreed. His greatness was not in controlling, but in empowering others to lead.

That is the same principle leaders must learn, whether running an army, a business, a school, or a family. You cannot carry everything. You must build leaders around you.

A LESSON FROM BUSINESS

Apple became a global powerhouse not only because of Steve Jobs' vision, but also because he built a culture of innovation where others could lead. When Jobs stepped away, Apple continued to grow because the systems and leaders he had developed carried the mission forward.

That is the measure of true leadership: what happens after you leave.

WATCH OUT

If the organization collapses when you step away, you are not leading. You were hoarding responsibility.

PLAIN INSIGHT

Leadership is proven not when you are in the room, but when you are absent.

CASE STUDY: PROMOTING FOR VALUES

I promoted people not just for their skills, but for their values. I wanted leaders who believed in the mission, who treated people with dignity, and who could be trusted when I was not present. Several doubted my decisions at first. But over time, those leaders became the backbone of the department. They carried the vision forward, and that is what leadership is about.

TOOL: THE SUCCESSION GAUGE

Ask yourself:
1. If I left today, who would carry the mission tomorrow?
2. Am I building leaders or just managing workers?
3. Do my people know my values, or only my instructions?

DRILL: DELEGATE AND DEVELOP

Pick one task you normally hold onto and give it to someone on your team. Allow them to do it their way. Resist the urge to step in unless necessary. Afterwards, review it with them and coach them through the outcome.

REFLECTION QUESTIONS

1. Am I still trying to do my old job, or am I focused on leading people?
2. Who are my right-hand people, and why do I trust them?
3. How do I know if I am building leaders or just collecting followers?

4. What responsibilities am I holding onto that I need to release?
5. If I walked away tomorrow, what would remain standing?

MODERN CONNECTION

In today's fast-paced world, leaders are constantly tempted to micromanage. Technology makes it easy to track details, monitor every step, and control every outcome. Leadership is not about control. It is about trust. Leaders build people who can carry the mission even in their absence.

That truth applies to corporations, schools, churches, and families. If things fall apart without you, you have not led successfully. Leadership is not about being irreplaceable. It is about being intentional in raising others to lead.

LEADERSHIP BRIDGE

I am not measured by how much I do, but by how many leaders I build who can continue the mission without me.

CHAPTER 7:
BRIDGING GENERATIONS

AT ONE TIME IN MY LEADERSHIP JOURNEY, an officer looked me in the eye and said, "Your way will not work for us."

At first, my pride rose. My instinct was to defend myself, to prove I was right. I realized this wasn't about method. It was about something deeper: generations colliding, each carrying different expectations, habits, and values.

That moment stayed with me. Generations are not labels. They are lived stories. If I want to lead people of every age, I must respect those stories and let them teach me.

Since then, I have heard the same clashes everywhere: in workplaces, classrooms, leadership platforms, national conversations, and even in late-night talks with friends. These themes follow me because they are universal.

WHAT WE MEAN BY GENERATIONS

When people hear the Silent Generation, Baby Boomers, Gen X, Millennials, Gen Z, or Gen Alpha, it can sound like a code. These are not codes. They are groups of people shaped by time, culture, and history.

THE SILENT GENERATION (1928 - 1945)

This group grew up during the Great Depression and World War II. They are often described as disciplined, hardworking, and respectful of authority. Many helped build the institutions, businesses, and civic systems that still exist today. The name "Silent" came from the idea that they were taught to keep their heads down, avoid drawing attention, and focus on sacrifice and duty.

BABY BOOMERS (1946 - 1964)

Born in the years of post-war prosperity, this generation experienced economic growth, the civil rights movement, and major social change. They are often associated with loyalty, consistency, steady progress, stability, and valuing structure and hierarchy. Many Boomers still hold leadership positions and continue to influence workplace culture.

GENERATION X (1965 - 1980)

This group came of age during a period of social and economic shifts. They experienced more divorce, layoffs, and uncertainty than the generations before them, which created a strong sense of independence and skepticism. They value honesty, balance, and practical results.

MILLENNIALS, ALSO KNOWN AS GENERATION Y (1981 - 1996)

This generation grew up during the rise of technology, globalization, and the internet. They are often seen as collaborative, adaptable, and purpose driven. They value feedback, opportunities for growth, and meaningful work that aligns with their values.

GENERATION Z (1997 - 2012)

The first fully digital generation, Gen Z never knew life without smartphones, social media, and instant access to information. They value authenticity, speed, creativity, and inclusion. They expect workplaces to be flexible and to embrace change.

GENERATION ALPHA (2013 AND BEYOND)

The children of Millennials and Gen Z, this group is growing up in a world shaped by artificial intelligence, global connection, and rapid technological advancement. It is expected that they will value empathy, innovation, courage, and leaders who demonstrate authenticity and care.

Not everyone fits the mold. I have met young people with wisdom beyond their years and older people who embrace new tools faster than anyone else. Labels are patterns, not prisons.

WHY GENERATIONS CLASH

The friction between generations is not new. Today, it shows up everywhere: workplaces, classrooms, churches, boardrooms, and even family tables.

- **COMMUNICATION STYLES:** Some prefer phone calls or face-to-face talks. Others expect quick texts or instant feedback.
- **RESPECT AND AUTHORITY:** Some believe respect comes with position. Others want respect earned through fairness and competence.
- **PACE OF CHANGE:** Some value stability. Others push for constant innovation.
- **DUTY VS. PURPOSE:** Some say, "Do it because it must be done." Others ask, "Why does it matter?"
- **FEEDBACK:** Some are fine with silence unless there is a problem. Others want consistent guidance.

- **TECHNOLOGY:** Some want time to adjust. Others expect tools to work immediately.

Left unaddressed, these differences harden into barriers.

BARRIERS AND TRUTHS: WHAT REALLY DIVIDES GENERATIONS

BARRIER 1: "THAT'S HOW WE'VE ALWAYS DONE IT."

Older generations see this as stability. Younger generations hear it as refusal to grow. *Truth:* Tradition matters when it serves the mission. When it does not, it becomes a wall.

BARRIER 2: "DO IT BECAUSE I SAID SO."

Many were raised to obey without question. Today, people want meaning, not just orders. *Truth:* Authority without explanation is empty. Purpose builds loyalty.

BARRIER 3: STEREOTYPING BY AGE.

Phrases like "Young people don't respect authority" or "Old people can't keep up" poison trust. *Truth:* Respect is not tied to age. It is tied to character and consistency.

BARRIER 4: "BACK IN MY DAY" COMPARISONS.

These often sound like criticism, closing minds instead of opening ears. *Truth:* Every generation faced challenges. The question is not whose day was harder but what we can learn from each other's days.

BARRIER 5: AUTOMATIC GENERATIONAL HIERARCHY.

Sometimes the oldest voice is trusted without question. Other times the youngest voice is followed because of technology. Both extremes fail. *Truth:* Wisdom and fresh vision must walk together. Merit is not age-based.

BARRIER 6: FEAR OF LOSING LEGACY.

Older leaders fear their work will be forgotten. Younger leaders fear being trapped in outdated systems. Both fears create resistance. *Truth:* Legacy is honored when it passes the torch, not when it clings to the flame.

BARRIER 7: STYLE OVER SUBSTANCE.

Too often the fight is about method instead of mission. *Truth:* The mission matters most. If the method works with integrity, style should not divide us.

BARRIER 8: CHANGE WITHOUT CLARITY.

Rapid change without explanation creates fatigue across all ages. *Truth:* Change without clarity is chaos. Leaders must explain three things: the reason why, the benefit of the change, and the timeline.

Generational differences are not walls to divide us but bridges to strengthen us. Wise leaders learn to pair experience with innovation. This is inclusive leadership, where the trait of respect opens doors between generations and makes every voice valuable.

TURNING BARRIERS INTO BRIDGES

Leaders can shift barriers into opportunities by:

- Naming them out loud. Admit when you fall into them.
- Reframing. Replace "Because I said so" with "Here is why this matters."
- Asking before assuming. Replace stereotypes with real questions.
- Inviting translation. Let one generation explain why an old method worked, and another explain why a new one might.

- Celebrating bridge builders. Highlight those who respect both history and innovation.

MY OWN LESSONS

I have learned from older voices and younger voices. I have also seen leaders dismiss voices outside their comfort zone. That is not leadership.

True leadership connects the past with the future instead of setting them against each other.

These insights are not tied to one job or one field. They come from years of work across education, law enforcement, community programs, and national leadership platforms. I have listened, taught, and learned from leaders of every background. The same concerns repeat everywhere. That is why I know these lessons are not just mine. They are universal.

WATCH OUT

Do not let age turn into a wall. Turn it into a bridge.

PLAIN INSIGHT

Trust, truth, and consistency turn leaders into bridge builders.

CASE STUDY: HONESTY AS THE TURNING POINT

A team stalled until one person chose honesty over comfort. That choice sparked trust, then momentum. Most turnarounds begin with one honest act.

TOOL: ALIGNING ACTIONS WITH VALUES

Each day note one action that matched your values and one that did not. Adjust tomorrow.

DRILL: BLENDING GENERATIONAL PERSPECTIVES

Pair two people from different generations to solve one task. Listen to both methods. Keep the best of each.

REFLECTION QUESTIONS

1. Where have I judged another generation instead of learning from them?
2. Who can I pair across age lines to create a small win this month?
3. What barrier do I use most often without noticing?
4. How can I honor the history of my team while still inviting the future?
5. How can I make my leadership universal and not just tied to my own background?

MODERN CONNECTION

In a fast world of short posts and quick wins, people still follow what is true, steady, and real. Consistency beats noise.

LEADERSHIP BRIDGE
I build bridges by telling the truth, keeping my word, and lifting others to stand tall.

CLOSING CHALLENGE

Generations are not enemies. They are chapters in the same book. My role as a leader is to make sure every chapter adds strength to the story.

The next time a young worker asks why, see it as a chance to teach purpose. The next time a veteran slows the pace, see it as a chance to protect the mission. Both are gifts. Both are needed.

Generations are not walls to climb. They are bridges to build. When wisdom and courage walk together, generations do not divide us. They multiply us. Be the bridge builder your team needs. That is how we build bridges across time. Every generation brings both wisdom and energy. The trait of adaptability allows leaders to honor the past while welcoming the future. The result is a culture where people of every age feel seen, valued, and needed.

CHAPTER 8:
OVERLOOKED LEADERS: THE POWER OF THE UNSEEN

WHEN PEOPLE HEAR THE WORD "LEADER," they often picture the CEO, the mayor, the superintendent, or the chief. They think of corner offices, boardrooms, or podiums. Yet some of the greatest leaders I have ever met never carried a title at all. They were the nutrition staff who kept children fed, the custodians who cared for schools, the bus drivers and crossing guards who children trusted, the nurses and technicians who carried the weight of patients' fears, the sergeants who built the culture of military units, the administrative and executive assistants who held entire offices together, the event staff who managed chaotic crowds, and the volunteers who built belonging in neighborhoods and churches.

THE NUTRITION STAFF

The cafeteria workers, now often called nutrition staff, are not simply handing out trays. They are handing out moments of stability to children who may not find it anywhere else. For some students, a school meal is the only reliable meal they will eat all day. The worker behind the counter is not just providing food, but safety, consistency, and dignity. When fights break out, I have seen nutrition staff step forward and end them with nothing more than their presence. That is leadership through presence, respect, and trust.

THE CUSTODIANS

Custodians, sometimes called building services or facilities staff, are often the first to arrive and the last to leave. They know the halls better than anyone, and they see what others overlook. I have watched custodians quietly intervene in the lives of students who were struggling. Offering a short word of encouragement in the hallway or a moment of correction delivered with fairness has the power to redirect a young life. Their leadership comes from relationships. They prove that leadership is about knowing your people and earning their trust.

THE BUS DRIVERS

Every morning and afternoon, transportation staff carry not just children but entire communities. Dozens of students may climb aboard, each with their own challenges, moods, and stories. Yet with a single voice, a bus driver can restore order. This is not because of authority alone, but because of consistency. Day after day, students know who will be waiting for them. They respect that steadiness. A bus driver may never call themselves a leader, but guiding children safely to and from school every day is one of the purest forms of leadership.

THE CROSSING GUARDS

Crossing guards, sometimes called traffic safety staff, stand in the rain, cold, and heat, ensuring that children make it safely across the street. To many, they may look like someone just holding a sign. To a child, they are a trusted guide. They greet families, encourage students, and build relationships in the small moments of daily routine. That is leadership built on faithfulness. They embody the truth that leadership is not measured in speeches but in showing up every day and protecting those who depend on you.

THE NURSES AND TECHNICIANS

In hospitals and clinics, nurses and technicians often do more leading than the doctors whose names sit on the door. They explain procedures, comfort patients, and carry the emotional weight of care. They are the ones patients remember long after discharge, because they were present in the hardest moments. Their leadership comes from empathy and consistency, qualities that inspire trust even in the face of fear.

THE MILITARY SERGEANTS

In the military, leadership is often seen as coming from the top, from generals and high-ranking officers. Yet every soldier knows that it is the noncommissioned officers, the sergeants and corporals, who shape discipline, culture, and trust. They are the ones who train, correct, and mentor. They may never be the face of the institution, but they are the foundation. Their leadership proves that respect must be earned through example, not demanded by title.

THE ADMINISTRATIVE AND EXECUTIVE ASSISTANTS

This is where shadow leadership lives. Whether they are called administrative assistants, executive assistants, or office managers, the truth stays the same. They organize schedules, guard the leader's time, manage communication, and often act as the first line of problem solving. They are the ones who keep leaders balanced and offices running.

Their influence reaches far beyond paperwork. A community may form its opinion of an entire office based on how an assistant answers the phone or greets them at the door. Leaders may carry the title, but assistants carry the trust. They are often the vital asset of leadership, quietly holding things together while others receive the credit.

THE EVENT AND STADIUM STAFF

At games and special events, guest services or event staff face angry crowds, long lines, and impatient voices. They keep order while showing respect. They are leaders in moments of high pressure, holding the line between chaos and safety. Without them, entire events would collapse. Their work proves that leadership is about creating order where others may expect disorder.

THE VOLUNTEERS AND EVERYDAY GUIDES

Beyond schools, hospitals, and events, countless volunteers carry unseen leadership. Coaches, mentors, ushers in churches, and community advocates build trust, guide young people, and shape lives. Their leadership is unpaid, yet it is priceless. They remind us that leadership in its highest form is service.

THE HEARTBEAT OF LEADERSHIP

What unites all of these overlooked leaders is that they do not seek applause, yet they carry influence. They are the steady presence that creates order, trust, and belonging. In most cases, titled leaders would collapse without them. They are the backbone, the heartbeat, and the quiet strength that keeps schools, businesses, hospitals, and communities moving forward.

WATCH OUT

Do not confuse being unseen with being unimportant.

PLAIN INSIGHT

Influence grows wherever preparation meets need.

CASE STUDY: ONE HONEST ACT SPARKS MOMENTUM

During a storm drill, the radios failed. A custodian who knew every hallway by heart took the lead. No rank. No title. Just preparation and calm. Students followed his voice to safety, and the staff never looked at him the same again.

TOOL: HIDDEN MAP

List three people without titles who carry real weight. Ask each for one improvement you will implement.

DRILL: ACCOUNTABILITY IN ACTION

For five days, end every meeting with who will do what by when. Follow up next day.

REFLECTION QUESTIONS

1. What am I doing that builds trust today?
2. Where am I leaning on a title instead of character?
3. Who am I raising to lead after me?
4. What cost am I paying that no one sees, and is it worth it?

MODERN CONNECTION

Online, the loud are rewarded. On a campus, the steady are trusted. Build around the steady.

LEADERSHIP BRIDGE

I honor quiet strength, and I move it to the center, because impact does not need a microphone.

THE CLOSING CHALLENGE

If you want to understand true leadership, stop looking only at the people with the biggest titles. Watch instead the ones who steady the room, guide the vulnerable, and carry influence without ever asking for recognition. Those are the leaders. They may not sit in the spotlight, but without them, the spotlight would go dim.

SHIFT: The Cost of Leadership, The Power of Change

PART TWO:
THE CLIMB

The higher I climbed, the lonelier it got. I kept climbing because stopping was never a choice. The climb is never as glamorous as people imagine. Each step upward tested my balance between ambition and sacrifice, between authority and trust.

    I lost people I thought would stay with me. I carried weights I did not know I could hold. The climb exposed me, challenged me, and forced me to grow. It also revealed what I was made of. Each step up came with a price. The question was how much I was willing to pay.

CHAPTER 9:
THE LONELINESS OF COMMAND

I WILL NEVER FORGET my first day stepping into the role of Chief. Like many leaders beginning a new chapter, I was not handed an organized playbook. There were no binders with all the answers or a smooth handoff of responsibilities. My test was to pick up where things stood and chart the way forward. Leadership often begins that way. Not with perfect clarity but with the weight of expectation.

I learned quickly that when you reach the top, the room gets quieter. Fewer people relate to your decisions. Some distance themselves because of your title, while others wait to see if they can trust your leadership before stepping closer. That silence is where the loneliness of command lives. It is not a punishment, but a test. It asks whether you can stand firm without applause, whether you can carry a vision when no one else sees it yet, and whether you can lead even when the cost is isolation.

Many leaders will face this silence in their own way. For a teacher it may be standing alone in a classroom with no support. For a business owner it may be carrying payroll when no one else feels the pressure. For a superintendent it may be guiding a district through change while critics wait to see you fail. Loneliness is not weakness. It is the proving ground where the trait of resilience is born.

THE RESISTANCE WITHIN

The loneliness was not just about an empty office. Stepping into leadership meant inheriting doubts and insecurities from those who wondered if I was the right person for the job. That tension is not unique to policing. Most leaders who enter a new role, especially from the outside, face it.

I chose not to bring in a new team from the outside. Instead, I invested in the people already here. I promoted based on values, not politics. Integrity mattered more than popularity. Over time, those investments paid off. The same people who once doubted me became the backbone of the department.

This is the universal challenge of adaptive leadership. New leaders inherit resistance, doubt, and sometimes hostility. The true test is whether you can respond with patience, clarity, and persistence until your values speak louder than your title.

THE WEIGHT OF LIABILITY

Loneliness in leadership is not only emotional. It is the weight of responsibility that no one else can carry.

When I sat behind that desk, I asked myself tough questions: Are we prepared for the unthinkable? Do our systems give officers what they need? Are our policies strong enough to guide us? The answers showed me where leadership had to begin. Training had to be strengthened. Policies updated. Accountability reinforced.

Those questions kept me awake at night, not because the team was failing, but because responsibility for readiness rests squarely on the leader's shoulders.

Every field has its version of this weight. Executives worry about markets, pastors worry about congregations, coaches worry about players, and parents worry about children. The burden belongs to the one in command, and it is carried in quiet moments no one else will ever see. This is the trait of accountability, where leaders accept responsibility others cannot carry.

DRAWING FROM EXPERIENCE

My one advantage was my background. Years with the Atlanta Police Department gave me a foundation in both enforcement and instruction. Retiring as an academy instructor meant I could teach, drill, and rebuild from the ground up.

With limited resources, I began training my officers directly, reinforcing standards and returning to the basics. I did not know who would truly buy into the mission, but I leaned on one anchor: the mission and vision were already here. I did not invent them. I believed in them. That belief gave me something solid to stand on while everything else was being rebuilt.

THE BLESSING OF SUPPORT

I was not entirely alone. District leadership listened to my requests and provided what was needed: uniforms, training materials, equipment, and technology. Partnerships also became lifelines. The sheriff's office deputized all my officers, giving them authority beyond school zones. Together we ran active shooter training, strengthening confidence and preparedness. Piece by piece, support and collaboration gave us the foundation we needed to move forward.

THE LONELINESS OF THE SEAT

Few see this side of leadership. You can be surrounded by people, yet feel deeply alone. The team shares success, but every failure rests with you. Yet, loneliness is not always a curse. Often it is a teacher. It forces you to lean on your values instead of applause. It teaches you to think deeply, listen carefully, and move steadily even when no one else understands.

That is why wise leaders create circles of trust. A mentor, a confidant, or a trusted advisor can be the difference between carrying the load and collapsing under it. This is relational leadership, where the strength of your connections keeps the loneliness of command from turning into despair.

BUILDING FROM SCRATCH

Leadership required me to strengthen foundations. Evidence procedures, training protocols, and policies all needed structure and clarity. These foundations are not glamorous, but they are necessary. They are laid brick by brick, often unseen until a crisis reveals their importance.

LESSONS BEYOND POLICING

History reminds us of this truth. Abraham Lincoln faced doubt and division even within his own cabinet, yet his persistence preserved the Union. Howard Schultz returned to Starbucks when the brand was faltering. He met resistance at first. By returning to the basics of quality and culture, he rebuilt the company's foundation.

Their stories prove that loneliness in leadership is not a mark of failure, but of vision.

WATCH OUT

Do not mistake loneliness for failure. Sometimes it is the clearest evidence you are walking a path no one else has traveled.

PLAIN INSIGHT

The higher the position, the smaller the circle.

CASE STUDY: BUILDING A TEAM FROM THE GROUND UP

There was no playbook waiting for me. My choice was simple: complain about what was missing or build up what was needed. I chose to build.

I promoted leaders who carried the mission, not just the workload. I made sure the team could speak about the mission and vision clearly, and more importantly, live it. Clarity gave us direction. Without it, the loneliness of command could have turned into despair. With it, the department began to move forward with purpose.

The same is true in every field. Purpose steadies the heart when applause is absent. Leaders anchored in values outlast storms and silence. This is values-based leadership, where vision becomes your companion when the room feels empty.

TOOL: THE CIRCLE OF TRUST

Identify three people inside your organization and three people outside your organization you can trust. These are the people you can talk to, lean on, and process challenges with. The wider the circle, the less lonely the seat becomes.

DRILL: BUILD YOUR FOUNDATION

List the systems, policies, or structures in your organization that are outdated, missing, or unclear. Pick one to improve this month. Strong foundations remove unnecessary burdens from leaders and create stability for the team.

REFLECTION QUESTIONS

1. What makes leadership lonely, and how do you handle that reality?

2. Who can you trust to support you when the weight feels heavy?
3. What foundations in your organization need to be built or rebuilt?
4. How do you ensure your vision is shared by those you lead?
5. In what ways can loneliness shape you into a stronger leader?

MODERN CONNECTION

Today's leaders face isolation in new ways. Technology keeps them constantly connected but rarely deeply connected. Many have thousands of followers, but very few authentic relationships. Surrounded by noise yet starved of trust.

The lesson is timeless: leadership will often carry loneliness, but the cure is building strong foundations, promoting leaders who share the mission and vision, and maintaining a circle of trust that keeps you grounded.

LEADERSHIP BRIDGE

I accept the loneliness of command, but I will not let it isolate me from my mission, my people, or my purpose.

CHAPTER 10:
TRUST EARNED TWICE

TRUST IS THE FOUNDATION of leadership. Without it, authority is empty. With it, authority becomes almost unnecessary. Trust is never fully secured. It must be earned twice.

The first test is competence. People want to know if the job can be done. If a leader cannot deliver results, provide direction, or meet the moment, confidence disappears. Competence gives you the right to be heard.

The second test is character. People want to know if you are doing the right thing when no one is watching. They look for honesty, humility, fairness, and consistency. Character gives you the right to be followed.

Leaders in most settings face these two tests. A superintendent earns trust when hired, but must earn it again when change becomes difficult. A CEO earns trust at the first board meeting, but must earn it again when the company faces crisis. The trait of consistency is what makes trust last beyond the first impression.

Fail either test and leadership collapses. Skills without integrity create suspicion. Integrity without skill creates frustration. Both are needed.

History gives us examples. Ernest Shackleton led his crew through one of the harshest survival stories on record. Trapped on Antarctic ice for months, his men trusted his ability to keep them alive. That was competence. They also trusted his fairness, his courage, and his willingness to share every hardship equally. That was character. Not one man was lost. Shackleton earned trust twice, and that trust saved lives.

The same pattern is visible in classrooms. Students test their teachers every day. Competence is seen in preparation, lessons, and knowledge. Character is seen in patience, fairness, and respect. Students may not remember every lesson, but they never forget whether they could trust the person who taught them.

Business leaders are judged in the same manner. Some achieve results that outlast them because they were built on both competence and character. Others push results at the expense of integrity and leave behind companies that fail when the truth comes out. Employees will work for a paycheck, yet they give loyalty only when they trust both the skill and the heart of the leader.

Leaders who pass both tests create legacies. Their influence continues after the title is gone because they proved their ability and their worth. Trust earned twice does not fade. It becomes the shadow of leadership that endures.

What I carried into the neighborhoods was authority, but what I lacked was credibility. A badge might open doors, but it doesn't open hearts. Credibility comes only from consistency, showing up, telling the truth even when it is uncomfortable, and refusing to let disrespect shake your respect for others. Leadership demanded that I live out the same standards I expected from the people I served. That is where trust begins, not in speeches or directives, but in daily actions that prove you mean what you say.

TRUST BEYOND AUTHORITY

Authority can be handed to you in an instant. A badge, a title, a corner office, or a promotion puts power in your hands. However, authority alone will never bring trust. Trust must be earned twice. First by keeping promises, then by enforcing accountability.

Over time, I realized that rebuilding trust was less about what the community thought of me and more about how I chose to lead in the face of resistance. Each encounter was a test of patience, humility, and discipline. People may not embrace you right away, but they will measure your character. In the end, authority without trust is fragile, but leadership grounded in character has the power to change even the hardest environments.

THE ACCOUNTABILITY FACTOR

Trust in the community will never exist if there is no accountability within the organization. You cannot demand trust from the public if you excuse failure inside your own house.

That is why I deal with issues immediately. If I hear about a complaint against an officer or supervisor, I do not let it fester. I bring the person in and deal with it head-on. Gossip corrodes organizations. Lingering problems turn small cracks into large fractures. Accountability must be direct and prompt.

For me, accountability goes beyond correcting behavior. It is about watching whether a person can set aside their ego long enough to self-reflect. If someone can honestly ask themselves, "Is there any truth in this complaint?", and demonstrates actions towards change, then they show me they are capable of growth. Ego is one of the greatest enemies of leadership. It blinds us to our flaws and locks us into failure.

I used to call these "difficult conversations." They were uncomfortable. No one likes confronting people they work with. I learned that when you address problems quickly and fairly, they lose their sting. Today, I no longer call them difficult. I call them necessary. Accountability handled with fairness builds trust not only inside the department, but also outside in the community.

A LESSON FROM HISTORY

Theodore Roosevelt understood this when he became police commissioner of New York City in the 1890s. Reports suggested that corruption was rampant. Some officers were accused of taking bribes or ignoring crime. Roosevelt did not just give speeches about integrity. He walked the precincts at night when officers thought no one was watching. He showed up in places where authority rarely went. By demanding accountability, he sent a clear message that integrity mattered more than appearances. Trust was rebuilt with consistent action rather than slogans.

A LESSON FROM BUSINESS

This principle extends far beyond law enforcement. In 1982, Johnson & Johnson faced the Tylenol crisis when several bottles of medicine had been tampered with, leading to deaths. The company could have minimized the issue to save money. Instead, they pulled every bottle of Tylenol off the shelves nationwide. The decision cost them millions, but it preserved trust. Decades later, that act of corporate accountability is still taught in business schools as one of the best examples of integrity under pressure.

WATCH OUT

You cannot demand trust while excusing failure within your own walls. The community sees through it, and your organization loses credibility.

PLAIN INSIGHT

Trust is earned twice: once by keeping your promises, and again by holding people accountable when warranted.

CASE STUDY: OWNING MISTAKES BUILDS TRUST

A lieutenant approved a schedule change that hurt families. He owned it in writing, reversed course, and ate the overtime to cover the gap. The unit trusted him more after the mistake than before it, because he paid the cost himself.

TOOL: THE TRUST TEST

Ask yourself three questions:

1. Do the people I serve trust me enough to call me when they are in trouble?
2. Do the people I lead trust me enough to tell me the truth, even when it hurts?
3. Do I hold my team accountable in ways that protect both them and the people we serve?

DRILL: PRACTICE RADICAL CONSISTENCY

Pick one promise you make to your team or your community this month. Keep it, no matter what. Small promises build the foundation for major trust later.

REFLECTION QUESTIONS

1. How have I earned trust in the past, and how have I lost it?
2. Do I see accountability as punishment, or as an act of integrity?
3. Who in my community or organization would say I am trustworthy, and why?
4. How quickly do I address problems when they surface?
5. What steps can I take today to strengthen trust both inside my team and with the people I serve?

MODERN CONNECTION

Trust is under fire everywhere today. Citizens doubt government. Employees doubt corporations. Families doubt institutions. Students doubt schools. Communities doubt police. The thread is the same: trust is fragile, and when it is broken, slogans and public relations campaigns cannot repair it.

Trust is not rebuilt by hashtags or slogans. It is rebuilt by leaders who show up consistently, act with honesty, and hold people accountable when they fall short. The world is not looking for perfection. The world is looking for integrity.

LEADERSHIP BRIDGE

I will own the impact, not just the intent, and I will make repair my signature.

CHAPTER 11:
THE GOOD, THE BAD, AND THE UGLY

EACH PROFESSION HAS SHINING EXAMPLES, and policing is no different. The best officers are those who show up with integrity, humility, and courage. They perceive the uniform as a reminder of responsibility, rather than a source of power.

I have worked alongside officers who went far beyond the call of duty. I remember the ones who stayed late after exhausting shifts just to make sure a child got home safely. I remember officers who quietly reached into their own pockets to buy groceries for families in need. These stories rarely made the news, but changed lives daily. They are vital to policing, and their work is what keeps the profession honorable.

THE GOOD

I see this kind of noble act regularly. We have supervisors and officers who run mentorship programs for boys and girls. They take students camping, organize weekend outings, and spend their own money on clothing, food, and supplies for kids who might otherwise go without. One of our female officers created a mentorship program specifically for young women, giving them a safe space to grow and be encouraged. These people sacrificed their time away from their own families to invest in the next generation. This investment is not sought out to be televised or posted on social media. The ripple effect of this work will be felt long after we are gone.

The same truth applies in various fields. A manager who defends an employee rather than exploit them. Teachers who stay late to tutor a struggling student. Parents who put aside their own ambitions for the sake of their children. The good in leadership is quiet, steady, and powerful. True leadership often reveals itself in these unseen sacrifices.

THE BAD

Not every story is good. I have seen officers who let ego, frustration, or bitterness creep in. Some resisted accountability. Several ignored training. Others treated the community with cold indifference, as though the badge excused their conduct.

These behaviors may not always make national headlines, yet they erode trust. One bad officer in a neighborhood can undo the work of a hundred good ones. Parents do not separate their experiences between "Officer A" and "Officer B." To them, the badge is one symbol, and if one person abuses it, the entire profession pays the price.

The bad side of leadership is not confined to policing. Managers hoard credit for themselves while their team does the work. Principals enforce rules inconsistently, showing favoritism instead of fairness. Parents lecture about values but do not model them. Leadership usually collapses when ego rises above responsibility.

THE UGLY

The ugliest side of policing is when misconduct crosses the line into abuse or corruption. These are the stories that dominate headlines and shake public trust. They damage the reputation of the individuals involved and tarnish the work of officers wearing the badge.

What makes the ugly so destructive is not only the behavior itself, but the culture that allows it to survive. Silence, false loyalty, and excuses are as dangerous as misconduct. When leaders refuse to confront what is wrong, they enable the transgression to cultivate.

I have seen officers throughout my career who weeded themselves out because they could not meet the standard. That is the best-case scenario. I have also seen officers with bad behavior rewarded and even promoted. That reality is painful because it tells good officers that integrity does not always win. It sends the wrong message to communities that are already skeptical of law enforcement.

This is not unique to policing. Dreadful leadership exists in boardrooms, churches, schools, and governments. It includes CEOs covering up fraud; politicians who bend the truth for votes; pastors who abuse trust for personal gain. The setting changes, but the lesson is the same: when the ugly is ignored, someone pays the price.

A LESSON FROM HISTORY

The Watergate scandal of the 1970s revealed not just one leader's wrongdoing, but an entire culture of cover-ups. President Richard Nixon's downfall was not only about the crime, but also about the attempt to conceal it. History reminds us that the cover-up is often worse than the mistake itself. Ugly leadership corrodes institutions. The lesson is clear: when leaders hide the truth to protect themselves, the cost is typically greater than the crime.

A LESSON FROM BUSINESS

In the corporate world, Enron is the ultimate cautionary tale. Executives manipulated numbers, deceived employees, and misled the public. For a while, they looked untouchable. When the truth came out, it destroyed careers, wiped out pensions, and shook faith in financial systems across the country. The ugly never stays hidden forever. It usually resurfaces.

WATCH OUT

Do not confuse loyalty with silence. Protecting what is wrong is not loyalty. It is cowardice.

PLAIN INSIGHT

Good leaders build trust. Bad leaders weaken it. Ugly leaders destroy it.

CASE STUDY: THE POWER OF ONE OFFICER

In one of the toughest neighborhoods I patrolled, there was an officer whose actions had poisoned trust. Parents mentioned his name. Kids avoided him despite my presence. His reputation made my job harder, even though I had done nothing wrong.

That experience taught me an important truth: you are not only judged by your own actions, but also by the culture of the organization you represent. If that officer went unchecked, the community assumed we were all the same. I could not ignore it. Addressing his behavior was not about punishing him. It was about protecting the trust of the community and the reputation of the badge itself.

TOOL: THE LEADERSHIP LENS

When you look at your team, ask yourself:
1. Who are my good examples, and how can I highlight them?
2. Where are the bad habits forming, and how can I correct them?
3. Where might the ugly exist, and how can I confront it before it spreads?

DRILL: THE INTEGRITY CHECK

Create a monthly integrity review for yourself and your team. Ask: what actions this month strengthened trust, and what actions weakened it? Write it down. Face the answers honestly. Adjust quickly.

REFLECTION QUESTIONS

1. What is one example of "good" leadership I can model right now?
2. Where have I seen "bad" leadership, and what did it teach me?
3. Have I ever ignored "ugly" behavior out of fear or convenience?
4. What accountability systems can I put in place to protect integrity?

MODERN CONNECTION

Accountability is important. Today, acts of leadership are magnified. A single good act may inspire thousands. A careless bad act creates doubt. An ugly act may go viral and destroy decades of progress in a single moment. Social media does not forgive easily, and the microscope is bigger than ever.

LEADERSHIP BRIDGE

I will highlight the good, confront the bad, and never ignore the ugly. That is how real leaders protect the trust they are given.

Many leaders see this contrast. In classrooms it is the student who rises with responsibility and the one who resists it. In business it is the employee who thrives under pressure and the one who buckles. This is why emotional intelligence is a vital trait. Leaders must recognize both the strengths and the struggles of the people they guide.

CHAPTER 12:
THE PRICE AND THE PROMISE

LEADERSHIP IS NOT FREE. It comes with a cost. Leaders pay for it whether through time, stress, sacrifice, or the weight of responsibility.

For me, the cost was often personal. I was absent from family events, birthdays were missed, and endured long nights when my phone was never more than a few feet away. Leadership requires you to be present for others, while being absent from those you love most. Balance is rarely easy.

Leadership typically has a price tag. This cost is universal. A CEO laying off employees. A teacher pours hours into struggling students while their own children wait at home. A pastor tending to the needs of a congregation while their family silently carries unseen burdens.

The cost also appears in the weight of decision-making. Choices carry consequences. Do nothing, and you risk failure. Do something, and you risk criticism. Either way, the leader carries the burden. That is why leadership is not for the weak natured.

THE ECONOMICS OF LEADERSHIP

Economists talk about opportunity cost, the principle that every gain requires giving something up. That principle does not apply only to money. It applies to life.

When you give your time to lead, you give up rest. When you give your energy to your team, you give up energy that could have gone to your family. When you focus on today's emergencies, you may delay tomorrow's dreams. Nearly every yes is also a no. Saying yes to another late night at work is saying no to dinner with your family. Saying yes to constant availability is saying no to rest. Saying yes to every demand is saying no to your own health and peace of mind.

Wise leaders count the cost. They ask themselves, "What will this decision give me?" and "What will it take from me?" Leaders who pretend they can have it all end up exhausted, bitter, and ineffective. Leaders who embrace the truth of opportunity cost make hard but necessary decisions about what matters most.

THE HIDDEN COST: FAMILY

The heaviest cost of leadership is often paid at home. I wrote about this in *7 Bridges: A*

Father's Reckoning. That book was my attempt to face the truth of what my children experienced while I was busy serving everyone else.

I thought I was doing the right thing by pouring myself into the community. I saw young people who grew up similar to my upbringing and believed they needed me. What I failed to see was that my own children needed me too. By default, not by design, I neglected them while giving my best to others.

That is not just my story. It is the story of countless leaders. The pastor who saves a congregation but loses his children. The CEO who grows a company but grows distant from his spouse. The officer who protects a city but misses milestones at home. These are not failures of intention. They are failures of balance.

The hidden cost of leadership is real, and leaders must face it honestly. If we are not careful, the very people we believe we are sacrificing for may one day tell us that the price was too high.

THE PROMISE OF CHANGE

Beyond the cost, leadership is also about the promise. The promise is change. Leaders can transform organizations, communities, and lives. That promise is what makes the cost worth paying.

I have seen distrust in communities grow into partnerships. I have seen officers who once resisted accountability embrace it and become leaders themselves. I have seen broken systems take small yet meaningful steps toward order. Change is never easy or immediate. It is always possible when leaders are willing to endure.

THE LEADERSHIP TRADE-OFF

Leaders must decide if they are willing to endure in order to experience the promise. Some choose comfort. They avoid tough decisions, ignore festering problems, and cling to outdated ways. Others choose courage. They face discomfort, confront challenges, and keep moving forward even when it costs them.

The trade-off is often the same: pay the price or settle for less.

A LESSON FROM HISTORY

When Alan Mulally became CEO of Ford Motor Company in 2006, the company was losing billions. He made sweeping, unpopular changes: restructuring operations, demanding accountability in meetings, and forcing leaders to confront uncomfortable truths. It was costly. Jobs were lost, traditions were challenged, and critics spoke loudly. Those sacrifices positioned Ford to survive the recession that bankrupted other automakers. The price was heavy, but it showed that lasting renewal is never free. The promise of a stronger company was born out of the willingness to pay the cost.

NELSON MANDELA: FORGIVENESS OVER REVENGE

Mandela spent 27 years in prison under South Africa's apartheid regime. When released, many expected him to call for vengeance. Instead, he chose reconciliation, leading the nation toward healing rather than civil war. His leadership showed that restraint and forgiveness can be more powerful than retaliation. *Lesson:* True leadership is proven not by how you treat your acquaintances, but how you treat your former adversaries.

WATCH OUT

Do not underestimate the price of leadership. If you are not prepared to pay it, you will never unlock the promise of change.

PLAIN INSIGHT

In leadership, every yes is a no to something else. The only question is whether you are aware of the cost.

CASE STUDY: BUILDING BRIDGES IN A SCHOOL DISTRICT

New leadership roles begin with hurdles. Structures must be strengthened, resources must be maximized, and the mission must be made clear. Through it all, I chose to believe in the vision of protection and trust, even when the work ahead seemed daunting.

The cost is real. You will sacrifice long hours, make tough decisions, and experience the constant stress of accountability. Over time, your team will become more prepared, students feel safer, and the community will begin to see results. The price is heavy, but the change is worth it.

TOOL: THE LEADERSHIP LEDGER

On one side of a page, write down the costs of your leadership: time, energy, criticism, sacrifice. On the other side, write down the promises you are seeing—growth, trust, progress, transformation. The ledger reminds you that cost and change usually work together.

DRILL: THE SACRIFICE CHECK

Ask yourself: What am I willing to give up seeking change? Write it down. Then ask: What change do I want badly enough to pay that price? The answer reveals what kind of leader you are becoming because your sacrifices show your values. Whatever you are willing to give up is proof of what matters more to you.

REFLECTION QUESTIONS

1. What costs have I already paid as a leader?
2. Where have I resisted paying the price, and what has it cost my team?
3. What examples of change encourage me to keep going?
4. What sacrifices do I need to make today to create a better tomorrow?
5. How do I remind myself daily that the cost is worth it?

MODERN CONNECTION

In today's fast-paced world, leaders face pressure to deliver immediate results. Social media magnifies criticism. Communities demand progress. Employees expect instant solutions. Real transformation requires sacrifice and time. Leaders who chase applause often lose impact. Leaders who commit to the slow, costly work of change leave a legacy.

SHIFT: The Cost of Leadership, The Power of Change

LEADERSHIP BRIDGE
I accept the cost of leadership because I believe in the promise of change.

CHAPTER 13:
LEADERSHIP WITHOUT BOUNDARIES

LEADERSHIP IS NOT CONFINED TO UNIFORMS, boardrooms, or titles. It runs through countless parts of life. A father guiding his children is leading. A teacher inspiring a classroom is leading. A teammate encouraging others to push harder is leading. A CEO making tough calls is leading. The settings are different, but the principles are the same.

Leadership is influence, and influence exists everywhere. Individuals at any age or position have the opportunity to lead.

LEADERSHIP IN FAMILIES

The first place most people encounter leadership is in the home. A parent can decide whether to lead with patience or anger, by example or with excuses. Children observe more than they listen. A parent who says "do as I say, not as I do" loses trust quickly. A parent who models honesty, discipline, and consistency builds influence that will last generations.

I have seen children lead as well. I saw a young girl stand up to bullies on a playground, even when it made her unpopular. That act of courage inspired other kids to speak up too. Leadership is not about age. It is about choice.

LEADERSHIP IN TEAMS

On a sports field, leadership shows itself in sweat and sacrifice. I have watched athletes who were not the most talented still carry teams because of their determination. They dove for loose balls, stayed late to practice, encouraged others after mistakes, and in doing so, they lifted everyone around them. Titles like "captain" are important, but real leadership is revealed in the moments that require effort without recognition.

The same is true in workplaces. Often, the person without a management title shapes the culture more than the manager. They arrive early, help coworkers, and carry a positive attitude even in stress. Their consistency earns respect.

LEADERSHIP IN BUSINESS AND ORGANIZATIONS

In corporations, titles may open doors, but only trust keeps them open. History is filled with business leaders who rose or fell based on their character, rather than their job descriptions.

Howard Schultz, when he returned to Starbucks in 2008, closed every store in the country for retraining. That was costly, but it rebuilt quality and trust. Leaders who choose consistency and courage over titles and benefits understand that people follow character, not position.

The lesson applies far beyond business. Any organization, whether a school, a church, or a police department, thrives or collapses based on how leaders earn trust.

LEADERSHIP IN COMMUNITIES

Community thrives when ordinary people decide to lead. A neighborhood mother who organizes a safety watch; a coach who invests in kids after school, or a volunteer who cleans up a park, each proves leadership without waiting for a title. These examples remind us that leadership is not about the loudest voice, but about the steady one who chooses integrity when others choose comfort.

LESSONS ACROSS BOUNDARIES

Wherever leadership happens, the principles stay constant. Titles may change, settings may differ, but the foundation is the same:

- Integrity builds trust.
- Consistency builds credibility.
- Sacrifice builds influence.
- Service builds respect.

Leadership has no boundaries because influence has no boundaries.

A LESSON FROM HISTORY

Harriet Tubman is one of the greatest examples of leadership without boundaries. She was never elected, never given a formal title, yet her courage changed history. Risking her life repeatedly, she led enslaved men and women to freedom along the Underground Railroad. Tubman's authority did not come from position; it came from trust, sacrifice, and resolve. She showed the world that influence is born in action, not titles. *Lesson:* Leadership crosses barriers of gender, race, or rank and proves itself through courage and service.

SHIFT: The Cost of Leadership, The Power of Change

A LESSON FROM BUSINESS

When Satya Nadella became CEO of Microsoft, he shifted the company's culture from "know it all" to "learn it all." He emphasized empathy, continuous learning, and collaboration. His leadership shows that culture and character can turn around even the largest organizations.

WATCH OUT

Do not confuse leadership with position. A title may open doors, but it will not keep people walking with you once you enter through those doors.

PLAIN INSIGHT

Leadership that only works in one setting is not leadership. Real influence adapts across boundaries and proves itself in every arena of life.

CASE STUDY: THE VOICE WITHOUT A TITLE

I once worked alongside a teacher who had no leadership role beyond her classroom. She was not a principal, not a department head, not even an elected leader amongst staff. Yet her influence shaped the entire school.

She took struggling students under her wing, encouraged colleagues when morale was low, and stayed long after the final bell to help anyone who needed it. Other teachers quietly began to model her methods. Students from across the school sought her guidance. Without an official title, she became a trailblazer on that campus.

That is leadership without boundaries: when influence is so consistent and so genuine that it extends far beyond the job description.

This truth reaches beyond policing, classrooms, or companies. Parents lead in homes, students lead in schools, and employees lead even without titles. Influence has no boundaries. Leadership is measured not by your position, but by your impact.

TOOL: THE LEADERSHIP MAP

Draw a map of your life: family, work, friends, church, school, community. Write one way you are leading in each area, whether you realize it or not. Then ask yourself how you can strengthen that influence.

DRILL: LEAD IN A NEW ARENA

For one week, step outside your normal circle. If you are a manager at work, focus on leading at home. If you are a parent, focus on leading in your community. Leadership grows stronger when practiced in multiple arenas.

REFLECTION QUESTIONS

1. Where in your life are you leading without a title?
2. Who follows you because of your character, not your position?
3. What lesson from family leadership applies to your workplace?
4. What principle in business leadership applies to your home?
5. How can you carry your leadership across all areas of your life?

MODERN CONNECTION

Today, leadership is needed. Businesses face cultural change, families face pressures, schools face challenges, and communities face division. Words will not heal those problems. Real leaders will. Leaders who will step forward in humility, influence without demanding power, and who will model consistency when the world is inconsistent.

LEADERSHIP BRIDGE

I am not confined to one setting. Leadership without boundaries means I carry the same values into every room, every team, every family, and every community I touch.

CHAPTER 14:
SEEING BEYOND THE HORIZON

LEADERSHIP WITHOUT VISION is like a ship without a compass. You may move, but you are drifting. Vision provides direction. It gives people something bigger than themselves to believe in and to work towards. This is strategic leadership. The trait of foresight allows leaders to anticipate challenges before they arrive and opportunities before others notice. Success belongs to those who prepare for what others cannot yet see.

Organizations need more than goals. They need clarity about why they exist and where they are going. When people understand purpose, they find the strength to push through obstacles and keep reaching for something greater.

In business, if employees do not know the company's vision, they simply trade hours for a paycheck. If students do not understand the vision of education, learning becomes a chore instead of a pathway. If parents do not cast vision, children wander without guidance. Vision is a vital asset of leadership.

CASTING THE VISION

Vision must be more than words on a wall. It must be clear, compelling, and reiterated. A leader should be able to share it in a way that inspires people to see themselves in it.

Great leaders cast a vision by connecting it to everyday life. A coach does not just say "win games." The vision is to build discipline, teamwork, and perseverance. A business leader does not just say "increase profits." The vision is to serve customers with excellence and create products that improve lives. A parent does not just say "do well in school." The vision is to prepare children to thrive in life.

If the vision does not connect to people's lives, it will not last.

LIVING THE VISION

Casting vision is only the first step. Living it is what makes people believe. If leaders speak about honesty but cut corners themselves, the vision collapses. If parents talk about respect but model anger and neglect, children stop listening.

I told officers that our mission was to protect students and build trust. That sounded good, but it only mattered when they saw me living it. When I walked hallways, listened to parents, and treated students with dignity, the vision became real. Leaders must embody the vision every day, or else it becomes nothing more than a slogan.

This is transformational vision. Teachers shape futures by inspiring learning. CEOs shape futures by creating industries. Parents shape futures by raising children who lead with character. Vision is the spark that turns tomorrow into something different than today.

KEEPING THE VISION ALIVE

A vision does not sustain itself. It must be repeated, reinforced, and revitalized. People forget. Distractions creep in. Crises demand attention. That is why leaders must keep pointing back to the vision.

In organizations, this means starting meetings with the mission and vision. In families, it means reminding children of the values and goals you are building together. In communities, it means returning repeatedly to the purpose that brought people together in the first place.

The leader's role is to make sure the vision stays alive when the noise of life tries to bury it.

A LESSON FROM HISTORY

Anne Mulcahy took over Xerox when it was near bankruptcy. Instead of chasing quick fixes, she made painful cuts, listened to employees, and rebuilt trust step by step. Her story illustrates that leaders earn followership through transparency and tough but ethical decisions.

A LESSON FROM BUSINESS

Walt Disney dreamed of a place where families could laugh, learn, and create memories together. He saw Disney World in his mind long before the first brick was laid. When people questioned him, his response was to keep building. His unwavering vision created an empire that continues to inspire joy across the globe, proving that disciplined imagination backed by relentless execution can transform entire industries.

WATCH OUT

Do not confuse vision with goals. Goals are targets. Vision is the picture of the future that gives goals meaning.

PLAIN INSIGHT

A leader without vision leads people nowhere. A leader with vision gives people a future. This is inspirational leadership. The trait of hope transforms vision into movement. People do not just follow plans. They follow leaders who give them something to believe in.

CASE STUDY: LEADING A TEAM THROUGH CHANGE

A department faced a major shift in direction. The old goals no longer fit, and people were uncertain about the future. Instead of focusing on what was ending, the leader painted a picture of where the group could go. By creating clarity and showing how each person's role mattered, the leader helped the team look past the immediate disruption and toward the opportunities ahead. *Lesson*: Leaders who provide vision during uncertain times give people hope and focus.

TOOL: THE VISION MAP

Draw a simple map with three points:
1. Where are we now?
2. Where do we want to go?
3. What steps will get us there?

This simple tool works in business planning, family discussions, and personal growth.

DRILL: THE ONE-SENTENCE VISION

Write a one-sentence vision for your life, your family, or your team. Make it simple, memorable, and inspiring. Share it with others and repeat it until they can say it back to you.

REFLECTION QUESTIONS

1. What vision are you living by right now, and is it clear?
2. Do the people you lead know your vision?
3. How do you embody the vision in your daily actions?
4. What distractions keep pulling you away from the vision?
5. How will you keep your vision alive when challenges come?

MODERN CONNECTION

In today's fast-paced world, vision is more important than ever. Without it, organizations chase trends, families drift apart, and individuals live without purpose. Vision brings focus to a distracted culture. It is the anchor that keeps people steady when everything else is shifting.

LEADERSHIP BRIDGE

I do not just want to carry a title. I want to carry a vision. When the title fades, the vision is what will remain.

SHIFT: The Cost of Leadership, The Power of Change

PART THREE:
THE TEST

The test of leadership came when the crowd was gone, and quitting looked easier than standing. Titles do not protect you from the test. Recognition does not protect you either. The test shows up in the quiet moments when no one is clapping. It shows up when your mistakes echo louder than your successes. It shows up when the weight feels too heavy to carry.

That is when leadership gets real. That is when you find out if you are willing to pay the price. The real test was never on paper. It showed up in moments that could break me or make me.

CHAPTER 15:
THE CULTURE YOU CREATE

I QUICKLY LEARNED THAT policies do not shape behavior, culture does. In my career, I have seen habits that ran deeper than any rulebook. Officers were cutting corners, saying, "that is how it has always been done." Others treated the communities, students, and parents with suspicion first and respect second. They modeled what they saw. I realized culture could either be my strongest ally or my biggest enemy.

I once walked into a department where officers dreaded coming to work. They sat in roll call with their arms folded, waiting for the shift to end before it even began. Gossip thrived. Accountability was scarce. The culture was toxic, and it showed in the way they treated the community.

I have also experienced departments where the culture was completely different. Officers encouraged one another, shared ideas, and took pride in their work. Their respect for each other spilled over into respect for the community. People trusted them because they trusted each other.

Culture is invisible, but it is powerful. It shapes everything. You cannot always see it, but you can feel it.

WHY CULTURE MATTERS EVERYWHERE

Every organization has an environment of culture. Families, schools, churches, corporations, and sports teams all carry a culture. It is the unspoken set of values that drives how people behave when no one is watching. It is the atmosphere people feel when they walk in the room. Leaders shape it through what they tolerate and what they celebrate. This is cultural leadership, where the trait of consistency makes the difference between words on a wall and a way of life.

A school with a culture of kindness produces students who lift each other up. A business with a culture of greed creates employees who look out only for themselves. A family with a culture of respect teaches children how to treat others throughout life.

Leaders set the tone, but everyone contributes. You cannot escape culture. You can only choose to shape it or ignore it.

POLICING EXAMPLE: BUILDING BRIDGES VS. BREAKING TRUST

Few fields show the weight of culture more clearly than policing. Culture shapes how officers treat people, how communities respond, and whether trust is built or broken. I learned that silence in the face of wrongdoing is not neutral. It is a choice that erodes credibility and breeds fear. When leaders allow silence to rule, trust disappears.

The same is true in business, education, government, or sports. Silence is permission. What a leader ignores, people assume is allowed. The trait of courage is what separates healthy cultures from broken ones.

Real change came when the culture shifted. Officers began to listen, to practice restraint, and to hold one another accountable. Communities responded because they could finally see consistency. Trust was not restored through new policies alone, but through a new culture that honored respect and accountability.

LESSON FOR LEADERS

No matter the field, culture will either carry your leadership or destroy it. You can write policies, set strategies, and deliver speeches, but if the culture is broken, none of it lasts.

Leadership is not only about what you say. It is about what your culture proves every day.

This is authentic leadership at work. People may not always do what you say, but they will mirror what you show them. The culture you carry personally will be the culture your team multiplies publicly.

BUSINESS EXAMPLE: CULTURE EATS STRATEGY

In business, there is a saying: culture eats strategy for breakfast. You can have the best plan on paper, but if the culture is unhealthy, the plan will collapse.

Look at companies that thrive year after year. They rarely succeed because of a single brilliant strategy. They succeed because of a culture that values people, innovation, and trust. On the other hand, when culture turns toxic, leaders cut corners, accountability is overlooked, or bad behavior is rewarded, and the entire company eventually crumbles. Enron is one of the clearest reminders. Their strategies looked good on paper, but the culture of deception destroyed them.

FAMILY EXAMPLE: CULTURE AT HOME

All homes have a culture. Some homes thrive on respect, patience, and love. Others are filled with chaos, anger, or silence. Children carry the culture of their homes into schools, into friendships, and eventually into their own families.

As parents, grandparents, or guardians, we are culture-setters. We not only teach by what we say, we model what we teach. A culture of honesty at home creates children who tell the truth even when there are consequences. A culture of service at home creates children who see others as valuable. The culture you create inside your home often outlives you.

SPORTS EXAMPLE: TEAMS THAT WIN AND TEAMS THAT ROT

Talent can win a game. Culture wins championships. I have seen teams with all-star players fall apart because the locker room was divided. I have also seen underdog teams go further than anyone thought possible because the culture held them together. Coaches know this truth: skill without positive culture leads to chaos.

The same is true for leaders in each field. Talent matters, but culture multiplies or destroys that talent.

THE CHIEF'S LENS: LESSONS FROM MY OWN CAREER

I knew culture would either make or break our department. Policies could be written, equipment could be purchased, but culture would determine whether my officers truly lived the mission.

Changing culture is a slow evolution. It does not happen with one speech or one policy. It happens through consistency, accountability, and a shared commitment to something bigger than us.

A LESSON FROM HISTORY

Dr. Martin Luther King Jr. knew that culture would determine the success of the Civil Rights Movement. He insisted on a culture of nonviolence even when violence surrounded him. That decision shaped the movement's moral authority. Without that culture, the vision could have turned into chaos.

History shows us that vision without enlightened culture cannot survive. Culture is the soil. Vision is the seed. Without healthy soil, the seed never grows.

THE TURNING POINT IN POLICING

Policing cultural shifts are necessary to build and restore trust; not use of slogans, press releases, or new policies.

That means ending the silence that protects misconduct. It means rewarding integrity instead of popularity. It means building a culture where accountability is not feared but expected.

This is the shift I have spent my career fighting for: from power to service, from fear to trust, from silence to accountability.

A LESSON FROM BUSINESS

When Netflix faced the decline of its DVD rental business, CEO Reed Hastings did not just pivot the company to streaming. He reshaped its culture. He encouraged candor, innovation, and freedom with responsibility, creating a workplace where people could challenge ideas openly and take risks. That cultural shift positioned Netflix to dominate an entirely new industry, more than the technology itself.

That is the power of culture. It creates an environment where truth can be spoken, and progress can be made.

WATCH OUT

Do not underestimate culture. It will outlive your speeches, your policies, and your strategies.

PLAIN INSIGHT

Culture is not what you write on the wall. It is what people do when no one is watching.

CASE STUDY: THE BRIDGE SHIFT

Peter Drucker's timeless warning rings true: "Culture eats strategy for breakfast." Even the best-written policies collapse under a toxic culture.

As Chief, I did not change culture by rewriting every policy overnight. I started by setting expectations and modeling them. I promoted people who lived the mission, not just those with seniority. Slowly, the culture shifted. Students began to trust the police. Officers began to hold each other accountable. That is the true test of culture: when it shows up in the behavior of the people, not just in the words of the leader.

TOOL: THE CULTURE CHECK

Ask yourself:
1. What is the unspoken culture of my team, my family, or my organization?
2. Does it reflect the values we claim to believe?
3. How can I shape it through consistency and accountability?

DRILL: MODEL THE CULTURE

For one week, pick one value you want your team or family to embody: honesty, patience, or respect. Model it in every interaction. Do not announce it. Just live it. Then notice how others respond.

REFLECTION QUESTIONS

1. What is the culture of the environment you lead?
2. How do you know if your culture is healthy or toxic?
3. What behaviors do you reward, and what does that say about your culture?
4. What steps can you take this month to strengthen the culture around you?
5. How do you make sure your culture will outlive your position?

MODERN CONNECTION

In today's world, culture spreads faster than ever. Social media can expose toxic cultures in an instant, but it can also highlight healthy ones. A single video of an officer helping a child or a company serving the community can inspire millions. Culture is contagious, for good or for bad. Leaders who ignore it risk breakdown. Leaders who shape it with integrity create movements that last.

LEADERSHIP BRIDGE

I cannot control everything, but I can influence the culture around me. If I structure it well, it will outlast me.

CHAPTER 16:
CLIMBING THE LADDER WITHOUT LOSING YOURSELF

TITLES CAME WITH PERKS: doors opened for me, people stood when I walked into a room, and reserved parking to name a few. I learned quickly those perks did not mean respect. I saw leaders who climbed the ladder only to lose themselves along the way. Their influence changed. Their humility disappeared. Their family ties weakened. I knew I did not want to become that person.

Every field is filled with people who gained position but lost peace, gained status but lost purpose. True leadership is not just about climbing higher. It is about staying grounded. The trait of humility protects leaders from being consumed by the climb.

Leaders go through stages. First, you learn to lead yourself. Then you begin leading a small team. Later you may prime other leaders, and eventually step into executive leadership, carrying the weight of an entire organization.

Each stage demands something different. What worked at one level may not work at the next. Too many leaders fail because they keep leading the same way no matter how high they climb.

If you want to grow as a leader, whether in policing, business, education, or family, you must be willing to shift your perspective at every level of the ladder.

This is purpose-driven leadership. A superintendent may face the pressure of test scores, a CEO the pressure of profits, and a parent the pressure of provision. Yet the real test is whether the mission outweighs the applause. Purpose steadies leaders when success tempts them to forget who they are.

LEVEL ONE: LEADING YOURSELF

Before you can lead others, you must master yourself. This stage is about humility, integrity and discipline. If you cannot show up on time, keep your word, and control your temper, no one will trust you to lead them.

At this level, success is measured by consistency. You are proving that you can be trusted to carry responsibility, even when no one is watching.

KEY TRAITS AT THIS LEVEL:

- Humility to keep learning
- Integrity in choices
- Discipline in habits

TRAP TO AVOID:

Believing you are ready to lead others before you have mastered yourself.

LEVEL TWO: LEADING OTHERS

The next step is leading a small team. In policing, the position may be a corporal or sergeant. In business, it may be supervising a small group of employees. In education, it can mean leading a classroom or a department.

This level is not about showing off how much you can do. It is about helping others succeed. If your team fails, you fail. If they succeed, you succeed.

KEY TRAITS AT THIS LEVEL:

- Patience to teach
- Vision to help them see why their work matters
- Courage to hold people accountable

TRAP TO AVOID:

Doing everything yourself because you think no one else can do it as well.

LEVEL THREE: LEADING LEADERS

This stage is a major shift. Now you are leading supervisors, not just employees. Your influence is multiplied through the people you lead, which means your mistakes are multiplied too.

Here you must focus on systems, consistency, and trust. If you micromanage, your leaders will suffocate. If you do not set standards, your leaders will drift in different directions.

KEY TRAITS AT THIS LEVEL:

- Skill in developing leaders, not just workers
- Emotional intelligence to manage personalities and conflicts
- Ability to delegate effectively

TRAP TO AVOID

Ignoring culture. At this level, the culture of your organization will reflect the standards you set, or the ones you ignore.

LEVEL FOUR: LEADING AN ORGANIZATION

When you reach the top of the ladder: CEO, Superintendent, Chief, or Executive Director, you carry the weight of the entire organization. Every mistake will eventually land on your desk. Success will be shared, but every failure will have your name on it.

This level is not about being the smartest person in the room. It is about surrounding yourself with people who are smarter than you in their areas and trusting them to lead. It is about vision, culture, and resilience.

KEY TRAITS AT THIS LEVEL:

- Strategic vision
- Ability to inspire trust inside and outside the organization
- Courage to make unpopular but necessary decisions

TRAP TO AVOID

Isolation. The higher you rise, there will be fewer people who are genuine in their perspective. If you do not build a circle of trusted advisors, loneliness will cloud your judgment.

PROS AND CONS OF MOVING UP THE LADDER

PROS:

- Greater influence and impact
- Opportunities to shape culture and direction
- Legacy that outlives your position

CONS:

- Greater sacrifices of time, energy, and sometimes family
- Higher visibility and criticism
- Increased loneliness and pressure

Leadership is not about chasing titles. It is about preparing for the weight each level brings and being honest about whether you are ready to carry it.

THE SURVIVAL TOOLS FOR ALL LEVELS

1. **SELF-DISCIPLINE** – No matter the level, leadership collapses without personal accountability.
2. **LISTENING** – The higher you go, the easier it is to stop listening. The best leaders never stop.
3. **ACCOUNTABILITY** – Build systems where both you and your team are held to clear standards.

4. **MENTORSHIP** – Leaders need people ahead of them and behind them. Be a student and a teacher.
5. **BALANCE** – Remember that family, health, and personal life are part of leadership too. Success at work means little if you fail at home.

A LESSON FROM HISTORY

When George Washington was asked to become king after the Revolutionary War, he refused. He understood that true leadership was not about holding the highest title, but about shaping a culture that would last. His decision gave birth to a democracy instead of a monarchy. That is leadership at the highest level, choosing vision over ego.

A LESSON FROM BUSINESS

John Maxwell, one of the most respected voices on leadership, has often said: "the true measure of leadership is influence, nothing more, nothing less." That influence changes form at every level of the ladder. In business, the CEOs who last are not those who chase perks, but those who adapt to each new level of responsibility.

SHIFT: The Cost of Leadership, The Power of Change

WATCH OUT

Do not climb the ladder so fast that you forget the people left behind. Each level teaches lessons you will need later.

PLAIN INSIGHT

Surviving leadership is not about speed. It is about steady growth and adapting to the demands of each stage. The trait of integrity is what carries you safely upward. Without it, the climb may be quick, but the fall will be even faster.

CASE STUDY: MY FIRST PROMOTION

I thought I could still prove myself by being the best officer in the field. I quickly learned that my job had changed. My role was not to be the best officer, but to make sure my officers became the best versions of themselves. That shift in thinking changed everything about how I led from that point forward.

TOOL: THE LEADERSHIP LADDER CHECK

Write down where you are right now: Leading yourself, leading others, leading leaders, or leading an organization. List three skills you need to master at that level before you move to the next.

DRILL: PREPARE FOR THE NEXT RUNG

Pick one trait you will need at the next level: delegation, vision-casting, or accountability. Practice it this week, even before you are promoted. Growth comes before the title.

REFLECTION QUESTIONS

1. Which level of leadership am I at right now?
2. What traits am I strong in at this level? What traits do I still need to grow?
3. Have I fallen into any traps at my current stage?
4. How can I prepare now for the next stage on the ladder?
5. What kind of leader do I want to be remembered as?

MODERN CONNECTION

In today's world, people often want to skip steps. They want to jump from entry-level to executive in record time. Social media glamorizes titles and perks but rarely shows the cost. The truth is this: every skipped level becomes a weakness later. You cannot lead successfully at the top if you have not learned to lead yourself at base level.

> **LEADERSHIP BRIDGE**
> I cannot promise that the climb will be easy. However, I can promise that if you grow at every level, the person you become will be strong enough to carry the weight when you reach the top.

CHAPTER 17:
LEADING FROM A WHOLE HEART

LEADERSHIP CHALLENGED ME to my core more than once. I carried grief, stress, and anger, yet had to lead others with a calm demeanor. The hardest moments were not solved by toughness, but by compassion. I realized leading with authenticity means embracing both strength and vulnerability.

Leadership begins within. Too many leaders try to pour into others while leading from a place of emptiness, pain, or unresolved trauma. The truth is, you cannot lead people toward wholeness if you are broken. Titles and promotions may cover it for a while, but the cracks will eventually show. The best leaders are not those who hide their wounds, but those who have done the work to heal them.

Throughout my leadership journey, I have seen leaders at all levels: teachers, officers, executives, and pastors, struggle because they never dealt with their own pain. They carried childhood trauma, abandonment, or neglect into adulthood. They buried their struggles under long hours, accomplishments, or control. When stress mounted or crises came, those unhealed wounds resurfaced. Some numbed themselves with alcohol, drugs, or affairs. Others isolated themselves, even while surrounded by success.

We see it in wealthy entertainers, athletes, and executives who seem to have everything, money, fame, and influence, yet end their lives by suicide or destroy themselves through addiction. Their stories remind us that emotional and spiritual well-being cannot be bought. If you are not complete inside, no amount of success outside will satisfy you.

It is essential to learn to lead yourself before leading others. Before you demand accountability from your team, hold yourself accountable to healing. If you carry trauma from your past, it will follow you into the present and shape your future until you face it. The most dangerous wounds are the ones we pretend are not there. Leadership is not about perfection. It is about courage. One of the greatest acts of courage is to ask for help, admit your pain, and begin healing.

THE DANGER OF UNRESOLVED PAIN

Unresolved pain does not stop with the person. In leadership, it leaks into nearly every decision, every relationship, and every team. Anger turns into harshness. Loneliness clings to authority. Abandonment pushes people away. The wound that begins inside the leader becomes a wound the organization must carry.

THE POWER OF THE PRESENT

Too many people live trapped in the past or anxious about the future. They replay old wounds, failures, or betrayals instead of facing the moment in front of them. Others worry endlessly about what might happen tomorrow, missing the gift of today. Leadership requires intentional presence. If you cannot lead yourself in the present, you cannot lead others into the future. Healing requires courage to face right now, not someday.

WATCH OUT

Do not lead from a wound you refuse to name.

SHIFT: The Cost of Leadership, The Power of Change

PLAIN INSIGHT

Strength without tenderness becomes distance.

CASE STUDY: FROM BURDEN TO BUY-IN

A respected sergeant carried grief that hardened into short tempers. He began weekly walks with a peer and one private counseling session a month. The tone of his squad changed. Their performance rose with their trust. Healing traveled faster than orders.

TOOL: THE LEADER'S DAILY WELL-BEING CARD

Keep this checklist in your pocket, on your desk, or by your bed. Review it daily as a reminder that your health is your first leadership responsibility.

✔ Did I pause for presence today?
✔ Did I have one honest check-in with someone I trust?
✔ Did I protect a sacred hour for family or renewal?
✔ Did I write down three things I am grateful for?
✔ Did I invest in one moment of joy today?

DRILL: SHARING TRUTHS

Choose one person you trust. Share one truth you have not said out loud. Ask them to check on you in seven days.

REFLECTION QUESTIONS

1. What unresolved pain am I carrying into my leadership?
2. How do my past wounds show up in my present leadership?
3. Who can I trust to walk with me in my healing?
4. Which daily practice will I commit to this week?
5. What steps do I need to take to lead from wholeness instead of emptiness?

MODERN CONNECTION

Currently, society rewards achievement but rarely inquires about wholeness. Leaders are praised for profit margins, promotions, and public recognition, yet frequently, their inner realm is ignored. That is why so many reach the top with a sense of being incomplete.

The shift begins with small, intentional practices that protect well-being. Here are five daily habits every leader can build:

1. **PAUSE FOR PRESENCE** – Begin each day with five minutes of silence, meditation, or prayer. No phone, no distractions. Just breathe, reflect, and remind yourself that today matters more than yesterday's regrets or tomorrow's worries.
2. **ONE HONEST CHECK-IN** – Choose one trusted person in your circle—a spouse, a mentor, or a friend—and be real about how you are doing. Honesty shared aloud breaks the power of hidden struggles.
3. **PROTECT A SACRED HOUR** – Block one hour each day that work cannot touch. Use it for family, exercise, or personal renewal. Guard it the way you would guard a critical meeting on your calendar.
4. **LEAD WITH GRATITUDE** – Write down three things you are grateful for prior to going to bed. Gratitude shifts focus from what is missing to what is present. It rewires your mind to see hope even amongst stress.
5. **INVEST IN SMALL JOYS** – Leadership can feel heavy, but joy preserves humanity. Listen to music, walk outside, laugh with your children, or read something that inspires you. These moments may seem small, but they remind you that life is bigger than the weight of leadership.

Leaders who practice these five habits daily build resilience. They lead not from exhaustion, but from overflow. They give not from emptiness, but from wholeness.

LEADERSHIP BRIDGE

I cannot lead others to healing if I refuse to heal myself. The strongest leaders are not the ones without scars, but the ones who have turned their scars into bridges for others to walk across.

CHAPTER 18:
CARRYING THE LOAD

LEADERSHIP OFTEN FELT LIKE A WEIGHT strapped to my back. Every decision, every complaint, every crisis landed on my shoulders. There were nights I lay awake wondering if the load would ever lighten. I learned that carrying the load was not about strength alone; it was about building systems and sharing responsibility.

Leadership is often spoken about in terms of vision, strategy, and outcomes. What rarely gets spoken about is the weight that ordinary workers carry every single day. Behind every company's success, or every community's progress, are men and women who give far more than they ever receive. They give their time, health, patience, and often their dreams. Many of them are not executive leaders. They are the people stocking shelves, teaching classrooms, answering emergency calls, flipping burgers, and patrolling streets at midnight. They are the ones carrying the load.

THE REALITY OF THE LOAD

In most organizations, those who work the hardest are compensated the least. They arrive early, stay late, and put their entire body and soul into work that is often undervalued. They sacrifice family dinners, weekends, sleep, and even their health to keep the engine of society moving. Teachers pour themselves into lesson plans only to struggle financially. Firefighters risk their lives for salaries that do not reflect their courage and bravery. Fast food workers and retail clerks keep businesses running while pondering how to pay monthly bills. Officers stand guard during crises, face dangers that are unimaginable, all the while listening to debates whether their efforts are even worth respecting.

When people are asked to give abundantly while receiving little in return, the risk is hopelessness and burnout. Hopelessness is the enemy of progress. Leaders who ignore this truth will eventually lead teams that stop believing in them.

WHY LEADERS MUST SEE THE WEIGHT

Leaders must ask a hard question: Do I truly see the load my people are carrying? Leaders cannot pretend that everyone has equal resources, equal opportunities, or equal recognition. Some carry heavier weight than others. The mother working two jobs to provide for her children carries a weight. The officer balancing trauma from work and stress at home carries a weight. The cashier who faces daily disrespect while barely earning enough to survive carries a weight.

When leaders refuse to see the weight, they become blind to the humanity of their people. When leaders are blind to humanity, they are no longer leaders; they are taskmasters.

THE CURRENCY OF RESPECT

Leaders may not control the pay scale. They may not be able to raise salaries or restructure benefits, but leaders typically control respect. Respect is the currency that multiplies effort. It costs nothing, yet it changes everything.

A worker who feels unseen will eventually give up. A worker who feels respected will give more of themselves than their paycheck could ever reflect. Recognition, a word of encouragement, a genuine thank you, or public acknowledgment of sacrifice, are small actions that have massive impact. Leaders who place emphasis on respect create cultures where one can breathe easier, even under heavy loads.

MOVING BEYOND THE PAYCHECK

The paycheck is important, and we should not pretend otherwise. However, money alone does not inspire. When a leader ties work to purpose, the load feels lighter. A janitor in a hospital is more than cleaning floors; they are sanitizing to prevent infections to save lives. A cashier at a grocery store goes beyond scanning items; they are helping customers obtain what they need to feed their families. A teacher is more than delivering lessons; they are shaping the next generation of citizens.

Leaders who frame work in terms of purpose lift the weight by showing that sacrifice has meaning. The question is greater than "What do you do?" The deeper question is "Why does it matter?"

WHAT HAPPENS WHEN THE LOAD IS IGNORED

When the load is ignored, morale collapses. People stop caring about quality, stop caring about teamwork, and eventually stop caring about leadership. Turnover increases. Cynicism spreads. Leaders may complain that their people are lazy or unmotivated. The truth is that people will not carry a heavy load for a leader who refuses to notice the weight.

SHIFT: The Cost of Leadership, The Power of Change

WHAT HAPPENS WHEN THE LOAD IS SHARED

When the load is noticed, recognized, and shared, something powerful happens. People rise. They push harder. They find pride in what they do. Leaders who step into the trenches with their teams show that they are not above the work but part of it. A CEO who spends time on the factory floor, a superintendent who walks the hallways with teachers, a manager who works a shift beside employees. These actions remind people that leadership is about both vision and solidarity.

LEADERSHIP INSIGHT

Leaders have a choice: ignore the load or share it. You may not be able to remove the weight entirely, but you can make it bearable. The true test of leadership is not whether people follow you when the load is light, but whether they trust you when the load is heavy.

WATCH OUT

Do not assume quiet means fine. Heavy things do not always make noise.

PLAIN INSIGHT

Shared weight builds stronger teams than shared slogans.

CASE STUDY: GRATITUDE

A dispatch center kept losing staff. The chief sat a full shift on the console to learn the pressure. He hired one floater, fixed broken headsets, and scheduled real breaks. The rumor mill turned into gratitude. People stayed.

TOOL: BURDEN BOARD

List every recurring task. Next to each, write the pain point. Fix one small pain this week.

DRILL: THE RECOGNITION LIST

Take one sheet of paper. Write down the names of every person you lead. Next to each name, write one specific thing they have contributed to the last month. Then, find a way to tell them you noticed it. A text, a note, a handshake, or public acknowledgment. This simple act lifts more weight than you can imagine.

REFLECTION QUESTIONS

1. Do I truly see the weight my people are carrying each day?
2. What non-financial ways am I showing respect and recognition?
3. How often do I connect my team's work to a deeper purpose?
4. When was the last time I stepped into the trenches with my team?
5. If my people could answer honestly, would they say I make the load heavier or lighter?

MODERN CONNECTION

Our culture applauds armor. Our people follow humanity. Leaders give both.

LEADERSHIP BRIDGE

I will protect people with a strong back and serve them with a soft front.

CLOSING THOUGHT

Leadership is not about standing at the top of the mountain and giving orders. Leadership is about climbing with your people, noticing who stumbles, and helping them carry what feels unbearable. When leaders carry the load with their teams, they create more than productivity. Strength, loyalty, hope, and values are created where people believe that their sacrifices are worth giving. This is how leaders transform workplaces and change lives.

CHAPTER 19:
PURPOSE OVER PAY

I THOUGHT ABOUT THE PAYCHECK, stability, and the benefits. The longer I served, the more I realized that money could never be enough to keep a leader going. What kept me steady in the hardest moments was purpose. The late nights, missed holidays, family events, stress, and pressure were not for a salary. They were for something deeper: creating a safer world for kids, families, and communities. Purpose is the fuel that outlasts a paycheck. Teachers stay in classrooms, entrepreneurs build businesses, and parents sacrifice daily not because of money but because of meaning. This is purpose-centered leadership, where the trait of conviction gives strength when pay cannot.

Money matters, of course. People work to support families, pay bills, and build a life. Money alone has never been enough to keep people inspired. Across each industry, from boardrooms to classrooms to factories, the greatest leaders know that the most powerful motivator is not the paycheck. It is the sense of purpose.

THE LIMITS OF COMPENSATION

Compensation can attract talent, but it cannot hold loyalty by itself. Even the best salaries lose their shine if the work feels empty, unfair, or disconnected from meaning. Workers who once felt motivated can grow bitter if they believe their effort is only fueling someone else's wealth. Teachers who sacrifice for their students, firefighters who risk their lives, or fast-food employees who put in long hours often know their paycheck will never reflect their full worth. Yet many stay because they feel their work matters. Purpose sustains what money cannot.

WHY PURPOSE MATTERS MORE THAN PAY

When people see how their work connects to something bigger, the load becomes lighter. A nurse does more than take vitals; she is extending lives. A janitor in a school is not just cleaning hallways; he is creating a safe space where children can learn. A delivery driver is not just dropping off packages; he is connecting families, businesses, and communities.

Leaders must help their teams see this bigger picture. Otherwise, jobs will feel like cages, and paychecks like chains. This is visionary leadership. When people are inspired by a mission greater than themselves, they will give more than money could ever buy. The trait of passion sustains leaders through seasons when pay is low and pressure is high.

THE LEADER'S RESPONSIBILITY

Although leaders cannot always control pay scales in some organizations, they can, however, offer purpose. That starts with clear vision. Leaders who only give orders are managers. Leaders who connect people to meaning are builders.

It is not enough to say, "This is your job." Leaders must say, "Here is why your work and performance matter." They must show that the contribution of each person connects directly to the mission, whether that mission is saving lives, shaping students, serving customers, or transforming industries.

GUARDING AGAINST EXPLOITATION

There is a danger when purpose is used to cover up injustice. Too often, people with a calling are taken advantage of. Teachers are told to sacrifice for children, while their pay remains stagnant. First responders are told to serve with honor, while their health is neglected. Employees are told to coexist as "family," while being treated as disposable.

Leaders who exploit purpose for profit destroy trust. Authentic leaders honor purpose while also fighting for fairness. They remind their people that meaning and dignity go together. Purpose is not a substitute for pay, but it is a powerful complement.

HOW LEADERS CONNECT PEOPLE TO PURPOSE

1. **TELL THE STORY OF THE WORK** – Remind associates what their role accomplishes. A factory worker should know how their product changes lives. A teacher should hear how their students succeed because of them.
2. **CELEBRATE CONTRIBUTIONS** – Celebrate the effort as well as the outcome. Recognize the unseen sacrifices.
3. **LINK THE SMALL TO THE BIG** – Show how daily tasks tie into the bigger vision. Leaders who connect details to destiny inspire perseverance.
4. **PROTECT THE MISSION** – Do not let vision get buried under profit margins or political games. Purpose must remain visible in every decision.

WHAT HAPPENS WHEN PURPOSE IS IGNORED

When work feels like just a paycheck, people clock in with their hands but leave their purpose behind. They do enough to survive, but never enough to thrive. They start counting minutes instead of making moments. The organization may still function, but it will never flourish.

WHAT HAPPENS WHEN PURPOSE IS ELEVATED

When leaders tie work to meaning, people give more than their job description requires. They innovate, sacrifice, and endure. Purpose makes workers resilient in ways money never could. It creates loyalty, creativity, and hope. People will buy into the purpose and want to be part of it.

LEADERSHIP INSIGHT

The paycheck may get people to the table, but purpose keeps them there. Leaders who elevate meaning above money create teams that endure, even in challenging times.

WATCH OUT

Do not rent hearts with raises. Win them with purpose.

PLAIN INSIGHT

Money starts the conversation. Meaning keeps it going.

CASE STUDY: TURNOVER

A security company doubled pay and still bled staff. When they connected every post to a person being protected, officers began to see names not just buildings. Turnover dropped without another raise.

TOOL: PURPOSE LINE

Write one sentence that links your daily task to a life you protect. Put it where you can see it.

DRILL: THE PURPOSE MAP

Draw a map with three circles: Task, Impact, Mission. For each role in your team, write down:

- **TASK:** What they do daily.
- **IMPACT:** Who benefits directly.
- **MISSION:** How it connects to the larger purpose.

Share the map with your team. Show them how their role is not isolated but essential. Watch how clarity creates energy.

REFLECTION QUESTIONS

1. How clearly have I connected my team's daily work to the bigger vision?

2. Do my people believe their sacrifices have meaning, or do they feel taken for granted?
3. Have I ever used purpose to excuse unfair treatment, and how can I correct that?
4. What story can I tell today that reminds my people why their work matters?
5. If money were removed, would my team still feel fulfilled by their mission?

MODERN CONNECTION

Metrics talk to spreadsheets. Purpose talks to souls. Use both.

LEADERSHIP BRIDGE

I will measure success by lives improved, not by hours consumed.

CLOSING THOUGHT

Leaders who chase profit alone may gain numbers but lose people. Leaders who elevate purpose create loyalty that no paycheck can buy. When people believe their work matters, they will endure hardships, overcome obstacles, and rise higher than they thought possible. True leaders know that while pay is temporary, purpose is eternal.

CHAPTER 20:
THE SILENT EXODUS: WHY GOOD PEOPLE WALK AWAY

I HAVE LISTENED TO PEOPLE ACROSS MANY FIELDS say the same thing: "I love what I do, but if another job offers more, I'm gone." I have seen applicants bring resumes filled with short stays: six months here, a year there, two years at most. Years ago, that would have been seen as a red flag. Today, it is common.

The truth is that people no longer stay just to stay. Many do not believe in pensions or in working the same job for forty years. They will not remain in places where they feel underpaid, overworked, or unappreciated. They would rather walk away than waste their time. Titles without pay do not keep them. Praise without fairness does not hold them. Empty promises do not fool them.

This is not just about money. It is about meaning. People leave when staying no longer feels worth it.

WHY PEOPLE LEAVE JOBS

Across industries, boardrooms, classrooms, and committees, I have witnessed the same reasons again and again. People leave for reasons deeper than a paycheck:

- **UNFAIR PAY**: When the cost of living rises but salaries do not
- **CRUSHING WORKLOADS**: When one person is asked to do the job of two or three
- **UNCOMPENSATED LEADERSHIP**: When people are handed responsibility without authority, support, or pay
- **EMPTY TITLES**: When the job description grows but the paycheck stays the same
- **STALLED GROWTH**: When loyalty is demanded but development is denied
- **TOXIC CULTURE**: When voices are silenced or ignored
- **A NEW MINDSET**: When people realize life is too short to settle for misery

There is also the matter of security. Many people do not stay because they love the work. They stay because they cannot risk losing their health coverage. Insurance becomes the tether that binds them to a place they might otherwise leave. Others remain because of children, grandchildren, or aging parents. Some stay because financial mistakes have left them with no choice. In these cases, the paycheck may cover the bills, but the benefits are what truly keep them in place.

I have listened to CEOs, executives, teachers, parents, officers, and corporate leaders describe these same truths. The message is consistent. People are not leaving because they lack toughness. They are leaving because they want to be valued.

THE FAMILY PARALLEL

This is not just a workplace issue. It is a leadership issue that shows up in families too. Children drift from homes for the same reasons employees drift from organizations.

- **AT WORK**, people leave when they feel underpaid or overworked.
- **AT HOME**, children leave when they feel unloved or unseen. Both are saying, "I want to matter."
- **AT WORK**, leaders pile two or three jobs on one person without support.
- **AT HOME**, children are forced to carry adult responsibilities with no guidance.
- **AT WORK**, leaders ask people to act as managers without authority or pay.
- **AT HOME**, parents enforce rules without building relationship.
- **AT WORK**, employees look for a new boss.

- **AT HOME**, children look for belonging in gangs, peers, or other households.

It is all the same stories. People will leave if they cannot find identity, respect, support, growth, and belonging where they are.

WHAT MY EXPERIENCE TELLS ME

I do not need to study to know if this is true. I have lived it, and I have seen it. I have worked in many fields. I have listened to countless voices: officers, teachers, executives, parents, community leaders. I have sat in boardrooms, in committee meetings, in classrooms, and in patrol cars. The details change, but the nature never does.

People want to be seen. People want to be heard. People want to be valued.

When those needs are met, people stay. When they are not, people leave.

THE EMPTY CHAIR

I often picture the empty chair. The chair at work that used to belong to a person who gave everything but finally walked away. The chair at the dinner table that used to belong to a child who stopped feeling loved at home.

Every empty chair tells a story. A story of a leader who failed to see, hear, or value the person who once filled it.

The cost of ignoring this truth is not just turnover. It is the loss of people who could have built something lasting if only someone had recognized their worth.

LEADERSHIP RESPONSE

Leaders cannot stop every resignation. They cannot prevent every family from drifting apart. But they can build cultures and homes where people want to stay.

1. Pay fairly when possible.
2. Respect always.
3. Be honest about workloads.
4. Do not hand out empty titles.
5. Support those asked to lead.
6. Create real opportunities for growth.
7. Build belonging that makes people proud to stay.

WATCH OUT

Do not let habits replace purpose. Lead on purpose.

PLAIN INSIGHT

Retention is a respect problem before it is a pay problem.

CASE STUDY: ACTIVE LISTENING

A high school lost three good counselors in one term. Exit interviews blamed pay. Stay interviews exposed the truth. They felt invisible to leadership. The principal began monthly listening lunches and solved two problems from each meeting. The exodus slowed to a trickle.

TOOL: STAY MAP

Meet with three solid people who are still here. Ask what would make them leave. Fix one item in seven days.

DRILL: TRACKING PATTERNS

Pull the last five resignations. Write the honest reason next to the official reason. Share the pattern with your team and your plan to address it.

REFLECTION QUESTIONS

1. Do I thank people only when they resign or while they serve?
2. What promise did I make that I have not kept?
3. How do I show respect without being asked?

MODERN CONNECTION

In a scrolling world, people stay where they feel seen. See them first.

LEADERSHIP BRIDGE

I will build a place worth staying, not a place hard to leave.

THE CLOSING CHALLENGE

Look at your workplace. Look at your home. Who might be drifting because they no longer feel seen, heard, or valued? What will you do about it before they leave?

The silent exodus is happening everywhere. In jobs. In schools. In families. People are walking away because they believe staying is no longer worth it.

The question is not why they left. The question is why we allowed the chair to become empty in the first place.

CHAPTER 21:
EXIT SIGNS

LEADERSHIP MEANS KNOWING when to press forward, but also when to step back. I have seen leaders ignore the exit signs until it was too late. They stayed too long, and their teams suffered. I learned that leaving at the right time is just as important as leading in the right way.

The workplace has exit signs. They may not glow in red letters above a door, but they exist in the language, behavior, and attitude of people preparing to leave. Sometimes the signs are subtle. Other times, they are loud. Either way, leaders who fail to notice them will eventually face an empty seat where a valued team member once sat.

THE MYTH: PEOPLE ONLY LEAVE SUPERVISORS

A popular phrase says, "People don't leave jobs, they leave management." There is truth in this. Poor leadership drives away good people. A manager who ignores, disrespects, or mistreats workers creates an environment no one wants to endure. But the phrase is not the whole truth.

People also leave because of coworkers who poison the atmosphere. They leave because the culture is toxic or uninspiring. They leave because the values on the wall do not match the behavior in the halls. They may also leave because of themselves. They carry patterns of discontent that no leader can fully repair.

SEEING THE REAL REASONS

Good leaders do not settle for convenient explanations. They ask deeper questions. Why did a talented teacher resign after only three years? Why did a dedicated officer burn out? Why does turnover keep repeating in certain departments? Leaders must learn to diagnose the real reasons people walk away.

- **SUPERVISOR-DRIVEN EXITS:** Stemming from neglect, unfair treatment, or lack of growth.
- **CULTURE-DRIVEN EXITS:** When the workplace feels disconnected from purpose, respect, or fairness.
- **PEER-DRIVEN EXITS:** When toxic coworkers make teamwork impossible.

- **SELF-DRIVEN EXITS:** When the individual brings the same dissatisfaction wherever they go.

Each category requires a different response. A one-size-fits-all excuse keeps leaders blind.

THE COST OF IGNORING EXIT SIGNS

When leaders dismiss departures as "just another resignation," they lose more than a worker. They lose knowledge, loyalty, momentum, and often the trust of those who remain. Resignations send a message to the team: either this is a place worth staying, or it is not.

The most damaging part of ignoring exit signs is not the person who leaves, but the silent ones who stay and give less.

HOW LEADERS CAN RESPOND

1. **LISTEN BEFORE IT IS TOO LATE** – Hold regular check-ins that are not about tasks, but about how people are doing. Many exit signs appear in conversations months before a resignation letter.
2. **TRACK PATTERNS** – One person leaving may be chance. Several people leaving is a pattern in the culture. Leaders must track exits like they track budgets.

3. **PROTECT THE MISSION** – Show that leadership values its people enough to fix problems when they surface. Action restores confidence. Excuses destroy it.
4. **CHALLENGE THE INDIVIDUAL** – When it becomes clear that a person is the source of repeated conflict across multiple jobs, address it directly. Leaders cannot rescue everyone, but they can hold everyone accountable.

LEADERSHIP INSIGHT

The true job of leadership is not only to bring people in but to give them reasons to stay. Recruiting fills seats. Culture fills hearts.

WATCH OUT

Do not explain away the signs. Read them and respond.

PLAIN INSIGHT

Absence has a voice. Leaders learn its language.

CASE STUDY: FEEDBACK LOOPS

A high-performing officer resigned. The exit interview revealed not pay, but disrespect and broken promises. The agency built a feedback loop and trained supervisors on follow-through. Retention improved.

TOOL: STAY INTERVIEW

Ask three people why they stay and what might make them leave. Act on one insight within seven days.

DRILL: THE STAY INTERVIEW

Instead of waiting for an exit interview, schedule a "stay interview." Ask your people:

- What keeps you here?
- What might cause you to leave?
- What can I do to make your work more meaningful?

Document the answers and act on them. When people see that their voice leads to change, they gain a reason to remain.

REFLECTION QUESTIONS

1. Do I know the real reasons people have left my team in the last two years?
2. Am I willing to face uncomfortable truths about my leadership if they are driving people away?
3. How often do I listen to concerns before they become resignation letters?

4. Do I protect my team from toxic coworkers, or do I allow poison to spread unchecked?
5. If I left my own workplace today, what reason would I give?

MODERN CONNECTION

People rarely quit in one day. They quit in little exits long before. Catch the small exits early.

LEADERSHIP BRIDGE
I will respond to warning signs with care and action, not with fear and force.

CLOSING THOUGHT

Exit signs are usually visible to those who pay attention. Leaders who ignore them will watch people walk away in silence. Leaders who take notice, address in real-time, and respond with humility, build cultures where people stay because their voice matters and have a sense of purpose. This is inclusive leadership. The trait of belonging assures people that they are not just part of a team but part of a family with a future.

PART FOUR:
THE RECKONING

"Reckoning comes when the truth shows up. The culture you built will speak louder than your words."

By the end, the titles do not matter. The applause does not matter either. What matters is the culture you created, the people you raised up, and the trust you either protected or destroyed. Reckoning is when the noise fades and all that is left is the truth about what your leadership really built. I had to face mine.

"When the dust settled, I had to answer one question. Did my leadership build bridges, or burn them?"

CHAPTER 22:
THE HAND-ME-DOWN PROBLEM

LEADERS KNOW THE RELIEF of filling a vacant requisition. The paperwork is done, the interviews are complete, and the position is no longer unfilled. However, what looks like a solution is the beginning of a new problem. Employees arrive with glowing references, polished resumes, and confident interviews, yet once hired, they display patterns of dysfunction that have followed them from previous employers.

These are the hand-me-down problems passed along by previous organizations eager to be rid of them. Instead of confronting the issue, those organizations disguise it, allowing another leader to inherit the consequences.

THE COST OF INHERITED PROBLEMS

When leaders accept hand-me-down problems without recognition, the cost is high:

- **CULTURE CONTAMINATION:** A single toxic attitude can poison the atmosphere of a team.
- **PRODUCTIVITY LOSS:** Energy is drained as others spend more time managing conflicts than performing work.
- **MORALE DAMAGE:** Good employees begin to wonder why bad behavior is tolerated.
- **LEADERSHIP DISTRUST:** When leaders do not address the problem, credibility is eroded.

It is unfair to the new leader, unfair to the existing team, and even unfair to the person, because avoidance never brings accountability or growth.

WHY IT HAPPENS

Organizations pass along problem employees for several reasons:

- Fear of lawsuits or negative press if the truth is documented.
- Desire to quickly fill a role without the trouble of correcting behavior.
- Leaders more concerned with short-term relief than long-term culture.

Instead of telling the truth, they quietly shift the issue, leaving another leader to discover what should have been revealed.

HOW LEADERS CAN RESPOND

1. **DO NOT ASSUME SILENCE EQUALS STRENGTH.** A glowing reference may indicate someone wanted them gone quietly. Leaders must dig deeper.
2. **TEST IN REAL ENVIRONMENTS.** Orientation and interviews reveal little. True character appears under pressure. Leaders should evaluate employees during real-world tasks before granting full trust.
3. **SET STANDARDS IMMEDIATELY.** Problem employees thrive in ambiguity. Leaders must establish clear expectations from day one.
4. **PROTECT THE TEAM.** Leaders have a duty to safeguard the health of the team. Allowing one hand-me-down problem to stay unchecked can cause good employees to leave.
5. **DECIDE QUICKLY.** Not every hand-me-down is beyond redemption. Some rise when challenged with structure, clarity, and accountability. Others resist. Leaders must know when to coach and when to release.

LEADERSHIP INSIGHT

Inherited problems are not a reflection of your leadership. How you respond to them will be. Strong leaders confront issues directly and refuse to allow another organization's avoidance to define their culture. This is adaptive leadership, where the trait of problem-solving keeps inherited issues from becoming permanent excuses.

WATCH OUT

Do not inherit a mess and then pass it down. Stop the cycle.

PLAIN INSIGHT

Inheritance is an option, not a sentence.

CASE STUDY: BREAKING THE CYCLE

A department inherited outdated tech and low trust. Instead of blaming the past, leaders named the problem, set timelines, and reported progress publicly. The cycle broke.

TOOL: CYCLE BREAKER CHART

List three broken practices you inherited. Repair one. Replace one. Remove one.

DRILL: THE RESET MEETING

When inheriting a new team member, hold a reset meeting. State your values, expectations, and vision clearly. Ask them to commit openly. Document the agreement. If they align, you have a foundation for trust. If they resist, you have revealed the problem early enough to act.

REFLECTION QUESTIONS

1. Have I ever ignored a hand-me-down problem instead of confronting it?
2. What safeguards can I create to protect my team from inherited dysfunction?
3. How quickly do I address destructive patterns before they become culture?
4. Am I willing to release someone if they refuse to align with values, even if they are skilled?
5. What message does my handling of problem employees send to the rest of my team?

MODERN CONNECTION

Heritage is a gift when it is healthy and a trap when it is not. Know the difference.

LEADERSHIP BRIDGE
I will honor what is true in our past and end what is harmful.

CLOSING THOUGHT

Leaders cannot prevent every problem from arriving at their doorstep, but they can prevent problems from spreading. Inheriting an employee is not the same as inheriting their past mistakes. Leaders who set standards and protect their culture prove that they will never accept dysfunction as a hand-me-down. The trait of accountability demands that leaders own both the past they receive and the future they create. Excuses may explain the problem, but only ownership provides the solution.

CHAPTER 23:
BEHIND THE SMILE

I LEARNED THAT LEADERSHIP often hides pain behind a smile. Many people perceived me as confident, strong, and calm. What they did not see were the sleepless nights, the stress, the worry about officers' safety, or the family moments I have missed. Leadership often demands that you smile through the storms so others can flourish.

Leaders have experienced the interview illusion. The person across the table presents themselves with polished answers, steady eye contact, and confident smiles. They seem like the perfect candidate. Weeks later, reality sets in. The person who impressed in thirty minutes cannot deliver in thirty days. At the same time, some of the most capable workers struggle in interviews. They stumble over words, fail to highlight strengths, or appear nervous, but when given a chance, they become the backbone of the team.

Appearances deceive. Leaders who judge solely by the surface risk filling their organizations with charm over character, polish over principle, and talk over action.

THE FLAWS OF THE INTERVIEW

The traditional interview is a performance. The interviewer asks familiar questions, and the candidate delivers rehearsed responses. The goal becomes less about revealing truth and more about surviving the test. Many skilled interviewees know how to play the game, while many great workers do not.

When leaders mistake interview performance for actual capability, they hire smiles instead of substance. This is true of principals, CEOs, politicians, and parents alike. Behind many smiles is stress, pressure, or pain. The trait of authenticity allows leaders to be honest without losing strength, showing that vulnerability is not weakness but connection.

WHAT LEADERS MUST LOOK FOR

True leadership hiring goes beyond the smile. Leaders must search for signs of:

- **CHARACTER:** Will they do the right thing when no one is watching?
- **HUMILITY:** Are they willing to serve before they expect to be served?

- **ADAPTABILITY:** Can they adjust when conditions change? ·
- **INTEGRITY:** When they make mistakes, will they learn from them?
- **RESILIENCE:** Can they withstand pressure without folding?

These traits cannot be measured by a perfect answer to "What are your strengths and weaknesses?" They are measured by how a person responds under real-life conditions.

STRATEGIES TO SEE BEYOND THE SMILE

1. **SIMULATE THE WORK.** Instead of only asking questions, put candidates in situations that mirror the job. A teacher should teach a short lesson. A manager should lead a mock meeting. A leader must see performance in practice, not in theory.
2. **CHECK REFERENCES THE RIGHT WAY.** Do not only ask former employers, "Would you rehire this person?" Ask, "What was the toughest moment they faced, and how did they respond?" Truth is found in specifics.
3. **LISTEN BETWEEN THE LINES.** Confidence in an interview is not proof of competence. Watch for inconsistency. Do their stories align with values, or are they designed only to impress?
4. **VALUE THE QUIET ONES.** Not everyone shines in the spotlight. Some are steady workers

who reveal themselves only after time. Leaders must learn to spot potential beneath nerves.

WHY IT MATTERS

The wrong hire is more detrimental than an open seat. A bad fit drains morale, damages culture, and creates more work for everyone else. A good fit can transform a team. The difference is not in the smile but in substance.

LEADERSHIP INSIGHT

The interview is a door that gives a glimpse of insight, not a mirror to see the complete picture. Leaders may choose wisely, looking past the polish to the core of a person.

WATCH OUT

Do not hire the smile and ignore the substance.

PLAIN INSIGHT

Charm can buy a moment. Character buys tomorrow.

CASE STUDY: PERSON VS. PITCH

A dazzling candidate told perfect stories in the interview. References were thin. Six months later, missed deadlines exposed the show. The next hire used plain words and had a line of people ready to vouch. Results followed the person, not the pitch.

TOOL: STAYING TRUE

Record one moment where you stayed true and one where you strayed. Use it to reset your direction for tomorrow.

DRILL: THE PRESSURE TEST

During interviews, create one unscripted moment that tests authenticity. Interrupt the pattern with an unexpected question or scenario. See how the candidate responds when they cannot rehearse. Often, the truth is revealed not in what they prepare to say, but in how they react when unprepared.

REFLECTION QUESTIONS

1. Have I ever been fooled by charm in an interview?
2. What steps do I take to evaluate character beyond answers?
3. How do I ensure I do not overlook quiet talent?

4. Am I willing to leave a seat open rather than fill it with the wrong person?
5. How do my hiring choices shape the culture of my organization?

MODERN CONNECTION

Influence culture sells highlight reels. Teams live in the footage between the highlights. Judge there.

LEADERSHIP BRIDGE

I will choose people I can trust on a quiet Tuesday, not just on a stage.

CLOSING THOUGHT

Behind every smile is a story. Some stories reveal character, while others reveal only masks and performance. Leaders who look deeper, test wisely, and choose carefully build teams that thrive on more than appearances. The right people may not shine in interviews but will excel in their work.

CHAPTER 24:
THEM VERSUS US

ONE OF THE MOST DANGEROUS mindsets in any organization is a 'them versus us' mentality. It begins quietly with conversations in break rooms or whispers after meetings. Employees start to believe that leadership is not on their side. Supervisors start to believe that employees cannot be trusted. A wall is built where a bridge should stand.

HOW THE DIVIDE FORMS

It often starts with a lack of communication. Leaders make decisions without explanation, and workers feel excluded. Small frustrations turn into assumptions: "They don't care about us." As the gap widens, employees band together for protection, and leaders circle the wagons in defense. What should be one team with one mission becomes two groups pulling in opposite directions.

THE COST OF DIVISION

When the divide hardens, progress slows. Workers do the minimum, leaders tighten control, and creativity dies. Loyalty disappears. Every Task feels transactional. Teams stop working for a shared vision and start working for survival.

No organization can succeed with an "us" and a "them" mindset. The future belongs to teams that see themselves as one. A divided team cannot win. Unity is not optional. It is essential.

HOW LEADERS BRIDGE THE GAP

1. **COMMUNICATE CLEARLY:** Explain decisions, even when they are unpopular. Silence fuels division.
2. **BE PRESENT:** Walk the halls, visit worksites, listen without judgment. Visibility builds trust.
3. **SHARE WINS:** Celebrate achievements as a team, not as separate groups. Everyone needs to feel ownership.
4. **MODEL UNITY:** Leaders must use language that reinforces connection: "we" and "our," never "you people" or "they."
5. **STAND IN THE MIDDLE:** Leaders are not above their teams; they are among them.

LEADERSHIP INSIGHT

Walls divide. Bridges unite. Leaders who fight against "them versus us" culture create organizations where people are not just employees but partners in a shared mission. Bridge-builders win trust across groups. The trait of fairness ensures that people know decisions are made with integrity, not bias.

WATCH OUT

Do not pick a side inside your own team.

PLAIN INSIGHT

We win together or we do not win at all.

CASE STUDY: REWARDING UNITY

Two campus teams blamed each other for missed calls. Leadership rewrote goals to be shared and linked bonuses to collaboration. The scoreboard changed because the rules rewarded unity, not pride.

TOOL: UNITY AUDIT

List your top three goals. Write how each goal requires help from another team.

DRILL: THE LANGUAGE CHECK

Record yourself in meetings or review your emails. Circle every time you use "I," "they," or "you." Replace them with "we" and "our." This small shift in language changes how people feel about leadership.

REFLECTION QUESTIONS

1. Do my words and actions build walls or bridges?
2. How often do I explain the "why" behind decisions?
3. What signals are my employees giving that reveal disconnection?
4. Do I celebrate wins with my team or take credit for myself?
5. Would my people say I stand with them or apart from them?

MODERN CONNECTION

Polarization sells. Collaboration protects. Pick the side that serves the mission.

LEADERSHIP BRIDGE

I will turn walls into tables and make room for every teammate to contribute.

CLOSING THOUGHT

Leaders who are team-oriented and embrace this approach turn organizations into families rather than battlefields. When unity is restored, progress follows. This is true in classrooms, corporations, and communities. Division drains energy. Unity multiplies it. This is collaborative leadership, where the trait of inclusion turns "them" into "us."

CHAPTER 25:
DO NOT FORGET WHERE YOU CAME FROM

I LEARNED THAT MY PRESENCE meant more than my words. Walking into a school event, standing beside an officer on a tough call, or simply being visible in the community, carried a message stronger than any speech. Leadership is not just about being in charge; it is about being present.

Titles change people. Promotion can be a blessing or a curse. Some leaders rise in rank and gain perspective. Others rise and lose themselves. They forget the very people they once worked with. They forget the struggles they once voiced. They forget the nights they went home frustrated by the same leadership blind spots they now repeat. This applies everywhere. A CEO who forgets the customers, a superintendent who forgets the students, or a politician who forgets the people will eventually lose influence. Humility is the trait that keeps leaders grounded when success tries to lift them too high.

THE DANGER OF FORGETTING

When leaders forget where they come from, they lose empathy. They stop listening to the concerns of frontline workers. They stop appreciating the long hours and small sacrifices that keep an organization alive. They see themselves as separate from the people they lead, and in that separation, respect dies.

Leaders who forget their roots often become the kind of supervisor they once criticized. The complaints they once made about unfairness, favoritism, or indifference now become their own habits. What they once hated, they now practice.

WHY PERSPECTIVE MATTERS

True leadership is not about escaping the bottom. It is about lifting others from it. Leaders who remember where they came from keep perspective. They understand that every role matters, from the highest office to the most manual task. They know that authority is temporary, but character lasts forever.

HOW LEADERS STAY GROUNDED

1. **STAY CONNECTED TO THE WORK:** Spend time alongside your team. Remember how it feels to be in their shoes.
2. **LISTEN TO THE VOICES YOU ONCE SHARED:** Value the insights of those doing the work you once did. They carry wisdom no policy manual can teach.
3. **REJECT ARROGANCE:** Titles should not make leaders untouchable. Humility keeps leaders human.
4. **HONOR THE STRUGGLE:** Recognize the hardships of your team as real and important, not as complaints to ignore.
5. **PROTECT YOUR INTEGRITY:** Never allow the climb to the top to cost you your soul.

LEADERSHIP INSIGHT

The higher you rise, the more important it becomes to remember the ground you started from. Leaders who stay connected to their beginnings lead with empathy, humility, and credibility. This is values-based leadership. Gratitude turns power into service instead of pride.

WATCH OUT

Do not cut the roots that kept you alive.

PLAIN INSIGHT

The higher you rise, the more you need your ground.

CASE STUDY: BACK TO OUR ROOTS

A chief went back to the block where he grew up. A grandmother asked, "Where have you been?" He started a monthly walk there. Crime tips rose. So did respect. Leadership went home and brought hope with it.

TOOL: ROOTS REMINDER

Write one story from your beginnings that shaped your values. Share it with your team this week.

DRILL: THE PERSPECTIVE WALK

Once a month, spend an hour with your frontline team. Do the tasks they do. Experience their challenges firsthand. Take notes on what you learn. Use those insights to make better decisions.

REFLECTION QUESTIONS

1. Have I become the kind of leader I once criticized?

2. Do I still listen to people at the level I came from?
3. How do I show my team that their struggles matter to me?
4. What habits keep me humble as I rise in leadership?
5. If my former peers saw me now, would they say I changed for the better or worse?

MODERN CONNECTION

Followers do not need perfect heroes. They need honest humans who remember why they started.

LEADERSHIP BRIDGE
I will climb without losing my ground. My roots will keep me true.

CLOSING THOUGHT

Leaders who forget where they came from lose more than memory; they lose credibility. The best leaders rise without losing their roots. They never stop appreciating the people who carry the mission every day. A title should change your responsibility, not your humanity.

CHAPTER 26:
UNLOCKING DOORS

WHEN I LOOKED INTO THE MIRROR, I asked myself one question: can I respect the man I see? Leadership has many rewards, but none means more than being able to face yourself honestly. Titles, recognition, and pay mean little if the mirror reflects compromise and regret.

One of the most destructive habits in leadership is when people hold on to knowledge like it is treasure locked in a vault. They treat wisdom as if sharing it would somehow make them smaller. That is not leadership. That is insecurity disguised as wisdom.

THE DANGER OF HOARDING KNOWLEDGE

I have seen it in policing. I have seen it in schools. I have seen it in boardrooms. People get promoted, gain a title, or reach a new position, and suddenly they stop sharing insight. They sit on information that could make people around them stronger. They keep quiet in meetings, or train just enough to say they did, but never enough to help someone rise to their level.

Leaders who think this way are building walls instead of bridges. They are blocking traffic instead of opening lanes. They may look powerful for a season, but eventually their influence shrinks because they were afraid to multiply it.

THE TRUTH ABOUT KNOWLEDGE

We have all heard the phrase, "Knowledge is power." But knowledge alone is not power. It is only potential. Power comes when knowledge is applied. Legacy comes when knowledge is shared. Knowledge sitting in your head benefits no one. Knowledge used can change a situation. Knowledge given to others can change a generation.

This is empowering leadership. The trait of generosity drives leaders to create opportunities for others. The legacy of a leader is not how many doors they walked through, but how many they opened.

TWO KINDS OF LEADERS

1. **THE GATEKEEPER:** Keeps the doors locked, holds back what they know, and measures success by staying ahead of others. Their leadership ends with them.

2. **THE BRIDGE BUILDER:** Hands out keys, lights the path, and measures success by how many others they helped cross. Their leadership outlives them.

Which one do you want to be remembered as?

WHY REAL LEADERS SHARE

Leaders who share knowledge are not afraid of duplication. They crave it. They want people to stand beside them, not beneath them. They want their team to know what they know, so that when the time comes, the mission is bigger than any single person.

Think about it: if your greatness depends on others staying small, were you ever really that great?

HOW TO UNLOCK THE DOORS

1. **TEACH WHAT YOU KNOW** – do not wait to be asked. If you have wisdom that could help someone, give it freely.
2. **MENTOR WITHOUT FEAR** – train people who might one day replace you. That is not weakness; that is legacy.
3. **CELEBRATE GROWTH** – when someone you train surpasses you, be proud. Their success is a symbol of the fruits of your leadership.

4. **CREATE PATHWAYS** – make the system better than you found it. Do not just walk across the bridge; make sure it is strong enough for others to follow.

LEADERSHIP INSIGHT

Leaders who hoard information become smaller with time. Leaders who pour into others grow larger than life.

WATCH OUT

Do not love the keys more than the people.

PLAIN INSIGHT

Access held by one is power. Access shared is leadership.

CASE STUDY: THE PIPELINE

A lieutenant kept every training slot for himself. When he retired, the well was dry. The next leader built a pipeline and watched leaders grow from the ground.

TOOL: KEY RING PLAN

List three rooms you can open for someone else. Commit one invitation this month.

DRILL: THE THREE KEYS

Write down three lessons you wish you had known earlier in your career. This week, pass each of those lessons to someone on your team. Do more than tell them, teach them how to apply it. Watch what happens when you unlock a door for someone else.

REFLECTION QUESTIONS

1. Am I holding back knowledge out of fear that someone else will pass me?
2. Have I created leaders, or have I just collected followers?
3. If I leave tomorrow, would my people be equipped to carry on without me?
4. What doors am I guarding that should be open?
5. What bridges am I building that others can cross?

MODERN CONNECTION

In a world that hoards access, generosity looks radical. Make it normal on your team.

LEADERSHIP BRIDGE

I will hold keys lightly and pass them often.

CLOSING THOUGHT

Leadership is not about being the only one with the key. Leadership is about creating more keyholders. The measure of your greatness is not how many doors you can keep closed, but how many lives you can unlock. The trait of legacy-building ensures that leadership multiplies. Great leaders measure success by who comes after them, not just what happens during their time.

CHAPTER 27:
ENOUGH IS ENOUGH

WHEN I PATROLLED THE STREETS early in my career, kids would stare at me in uniform. Some saw me as protection, others as a threat. For me, I saw myself in them. I came from similar neighborhoods, walked similar cracked sidewalks, and knew what it felt like to grow up overlooked. That background gave me an advantage many officers never had. I could build relationships because people knew I understood their struggle.

I stood on porches where families had lost loved ones. I broke up fights in schools where frustration and poverty boiled over. I sat with people who had given up hope, and I reminded them that hope still existed. Those years shaped me as much as the badge. They taught me that leadership is not about distance; it is about connection.

Here is the hard truth about leadership: some people stay long after their fire has gone out. They are still sitting in the chair, but their passion left years ago. They once came to work full of energy, but now they are bored, bitter, or just going through the motions. They stay because the check still comes, not because the calling still burns.

WHY LEADERS HOLD ON TOO LONG

I have seen it repeatedly, in every rank and role:

- Some stay because they still want the paycheck even though they are tired of the job.
- Some stay because they do not know who they are without the title, even though the job has become boring.
- Some stay simply because it is comfortable.

Whatever the reason, the outcome is the same: they stop adding value.

THE COST OF STAYING TOO LONG

When leaders overstay their season, the damage spreads.

- The culture sinks. People may begin to coast, and excellence slips.
- Younger leaders lose opportunities because the seat is occupied.
- Morale crumbles when hard workers watch others collect paychecks for doing the minimum.

- The organization begins to rot from the inside.

What started as a career of service becomes a dead weight on the very mission they once claimed to love.

KNOWING WHEN TO LET GO

Leaders need the courage to say, "Enough is enough." There comes a point when the right thing is not to hold on, but to step aside. Even if you love the work, there will come a time when it is no longer your season to carry it. Leadership is not about holding on to a chair until you cannot stand anymore. It is about building others, pouring out your knowledge, and letting the next generation rise.

LESSONS FROM THE STREET

I remember one night on patrol when an older officer came with me on a call. He had been on the job for decades. He sat in the squad car, staring out the window, and said, "Curtis, I do not enjoy this anymore. I am just here for the retirement check and health insurance." That stuck with me. His body was there, but his spirit had already retired. That moment taught me a lesson: I never want to become the officer, the supervisor, or the leader who is detached and loses passion for a position I hold.

THE BATON TEST

Leadership is like a relay race. You do not win by clutching the baton until the race ends. You win by running your leg with everything you have, then passing the baton clean to the next runner. If you hold it too long, the team loses momentum. If you pass it with strength, the mission continues.

PRACTICAL WAYS TO FINISH WELL

1. **BE HONEST WITH YOURSELF** – ask if you are still giving your best or just showing up.
2. **MENTOR THE NEXT RUNNER** – train someone to take the baton and run with it.
3. **LEAVE WITH DIGNITY** – stepping down is not weakness. It secures your legacy.
4. **CELEBRATE THE MISSION** – remember the "why" behind your work and honor it by leaving strong.

LEADERSHIP INSIGHT

True leadership is not measured by how long you stay, but by how well you finish.

WATCH OUT

Do not stay so long that you block the light for the next leader.

PLAIN INSIGHT

Finishing well is part of leading well.

CASE STUDY: LEGACY

A respected officer could not let go of a special assignment. A younger teammate stopped growing. When the veteran coached the successor and stepped out, the unit doubled its output, and he gained his legacy.

TOOL: SEASON TEST

Ask three trusted voices if the role you hold still fits you. Listen without defense.

DRILL: THE LEGACY LETTER

Write a one-page letter to the person who will one day replace you. Share what you have learned, what you wish you had done differently, and what they must carry forward. Keep it sealed until the right moment. This act forces you to think beyond yourself and focus on the continuing mission.

REFLECTION QUESTIONS

1. Am I still giving my best effort, or am I coasting?
2. Am I showing up with the same passion I started with?
3. Have I prepared someone to carry the mission after me?
4. Would my people say I am leading, or just taking up space?
5. How do I want to be remembered when I leave?

MODERN CONNECTION

Titles change. Seasons change. Legacy is how you manage both.

LEADERSHIP BRIDGE

I will leave room for new voices, and I will make the handoff a moment of pride.

CLOSING THOUGHT

Leaders who stay too long shrink their influence. Leaders who finish well expand it. At some point, enough is enough. The measure of leadership is not how long you can stay in that position, but whether you leave it stronger than you found it.

CHAPTER 28:
THE SABOTAGE WITHIN

SOME OF THE TOUGHEST BATTLES I see in leadership do not come from the outside, but within. You see people smiling in meetings, who then work behind the scenes to tear down progress. Sabotage is often quiet, disguised as "just sharing concerns" or "asking questions," but its effect is destructive. A team can survive outside pressure, but internal sabotage eats away at trust.

Challenges I faced in leadership did not come from the streets or outside critics. They came from the people inside my own team. The ones I mentored, defended, and supported were the very ones who tried to tear me down.

An enemy on the outside is easy to spot. You can prepare for it and meet it head on. Sabotage inside the department is different. It hides behind smiles, nods of agreement, and polite words. Later, it emerges in resistance, doubt, or flat-out betrayal. That is the kind of opposition that wears leaders down the most.

Over the years, I have had countless conversations with other leaders about this. It is not just something that happens in policing. Corporate executives, school administrators, restaurant managers, coaches, and supervisors at fast food establishments have said the same. They worked hard to be fair, supportive, and encouraging, but someone on their team still tried to sabotage them. It happens nearly everywhere. It does not matter the job, the field, or the position.

I remember leading an operation where every detail mattered. One officer never challenged me during the briefing or raised a concern. When it came time to act, he refused to follow through, which put others in danger. That was not a mistake. That was sabotage. It reminded me that leadership is more than creating a vision and moving forward. It is about protecting the mission from those who undermine it from within. Often, sabotage has nothing to do with the leader. You can be consistent, supportive, and approachable. Some people will resist no matter what. It took me years to accept this reality.

WHY PEOPLE SABOTAGE

- **JEALOUSY:** Some cannot stand to see someone else succeed, so they pull others down.

- **FEAR OF CHANGE**: New direction threatens their comfort, so they resist anything new.
- **CONTROL ISSUES**: They may not want the title but want influence. Sabotage becomes their way of holding power.
- **PERSONAL STRUGGLES**: Some are dealing with private pain, anger, or trauma that spills over at work. Their actions are not about you. They are about the burdens they are carrying.
- **SELFISHNESS**: Some simply care more about themselves than the mission, so they choose to disrupt rather than build.

Even when you take the time to explain why you are leading the department or organization in a certain direction, and most of the team is on board, there is usually one person who refuses to see it. They may not understand, or they may simply not want to. Other times, the resistance comes from a place of pain. You may never fully know.

WHO REALLY PAYS THE PRICE

Sabotage does not ultimately hurt the leader. A leader may feel the sting, may be frustrated, or must answer tough questions, but the actual cost falls on the people being served.

- When an officer refuses to work a game, it is the students and families who lose their sense of safety.
- When an employee in a restaurant refuses to give their best, it is the customer who gets poor service.
- When a teacher undermines their principal, it is the students who miss the stability they deserve.
- When a corporate team member resists out of jealousy or spite, it is the client or customer who pays the price.

People think they are hurting their boss, but are actually hurting the mission. The ones who pay the highest price are the community, the customers, and the very people who depend on us. Sabotage is more than a personal attack. It is a betrayal of service.

THE COST OF SABOTAGE

Sabotage poisons trust and slows momentum. It divides teams, creates frustration, and discourages those who are trying to move forward. Left unchecked, it can undo months or even years of progress. Leaders must recognize it for what it is and deal with it directly. Ignoring sabotage only makes it more toxic.

HOW LEADERS CONFRONT SABOTAGE

1. **SHINE A LIGHT ON IT** – Do not let whispers and hidden resistance stay in the dark. Address it openly.
2. **SET STANDARDS** – Make it clear that disagreement is healthy, but sabotage is unacceptable.
3. **PROTECT THE MISSION** – Remind the team that the mission is bigger than any one person's feelings.
4. **STAY STEADY** – Do not let sabotage distract you or convince you that you are failing. Many leaders face it.

WATCH OUT

Do not allow agreements in the room and attacks in the hallway.

PLAIN INSIGHT

Healthy teams argue to improve the plan and unite to execute it.

CASE STUDY: RETURNING PROGRESS

Two supervisors nodded in meetings and then rewrote the plan in private. The chief set a clear line. Debate here. Align out there. First violation meant a closed-door conversation. Second meant a public reset. Third meant a different seat. Progress returned.

TOOL: ALIGNMENT RULE

Put these words on the agenda and read them aloud every time. Debate here. Align out there.

DRILL: THE TRUST SCAN

Write down the names of your team members. Place a star next to those who consistently build trust. Place a question mark next to those who create conflict or doubt. Now ask yourself, "What action do I need to take to protect the mission and strengthen the team?"

REFLECTION QUESTIONS

1. How do I respond when I recognize sabotage?
2. Am I taking sabotage too personally when it may have nothing to do with me?
3. Who on my team builds trust, and who quietly tears it down?
4. How do I remind my team that sabotage hurts the people we serve most?

MODERN CONNECTION

Most missions are not sunk by enemies. They are sunk by friendly fire. End it.

LEADERSHIP BRIDGE

I will create brave rooms for debate and a single voice for action.

CLOSING THOUGHT

Leaders will face sabotage. It does not always mean you did something wrong. In most cases, it has little to do with you. It is about the struggles, insecurities, or jealousy of others. The louder your mission, the stronger the resistance will be. The most important thing to remember is this: sabotage does not hurt the leader as much as it hurts the mission. It is the community, the customers, and the people we serve who pay the highest price. A true leader confronts sabotage, protects the mission, and keeps moving forward with those who still believe. The trait of vigilance helps leaders identify sabotage early, before it destroys morale.

CHAPTER 29:
PRESENCE WITHOUT PERFORMANCE

I HAVE SEEN IT ACROSS MANY FIELDS. People sign up for a job, go through the hiring process, accept the paycheck, and then decide they do not want to do the job. They show up, but they do not engage. They ignore policies, cut corners, resist procedures, and complain at every turn. They still expect to get paid, but they no longer honor the responsibility they agreed to carry.

This is not just about laziness. It is about clarity of vision.

THE PROBLEM LEADERS FACE

For leaders, these employees create a unique burden. It is one thing to lose someone who walks away. It is another to carry someone who stays but refuses to work.

- **THE PAYCHECK MINDSET:** They believe presence is enough. They clock in, but they never buy in.

- **THE CONSTANT COMPLAINERS:** Their negativity drains energy from the team.
- **THE SABOTEURS:** Some do the bare minimum or actively resist policies, slowing down progress for everyone else.
- **THE SILENT COST:** Good employees see poor performance tolerated and start asking, "Why should I give my best if they don't?"

One unmotivated person can poison an entire culture.

WHY IT HAPPENS

1. **WRONG FIT:** Some people never wanted the job. They accepted it out of need, not passion.
2. **LOSS OF PURPOSE:** Over time, they stop believing the work matters.
3. **ENTITLEMENT:** They believe showing up alone earns a paycheck.
4. **WEAK ACCOUNTABILITY:** When leaders allow poor behavior to continue, it spreads.
5. **THE CLEAR VISION GAP:** Many employees never see where the organization is truly going. Some never hear the vision at all. Others hear it once during orientation but never see it reinforced. Some hear vague phrases with no practical meaning. Others see leaders talk about vision but act in ways that contradict it. Without a clear vision, work feels like

wandering. People drift, they disengage, and they disconnect from the mission.

THE CLEAR VISION GAP

A workplace without a clear vision is like a ship without a compass. People may row, but they do not know which direction they are going. That creates frustration for some and apathy for others.

I have heard people say, "I'll do what I have to, but I won't give more than the minimum. I cannot commit to something I cannot see."

Clear vision is what transforms a paycheck into a purpose. A blurred vision leaves people walking in circles, never sure if their effort matters.

THE HIDDEN COST OF PASSION

There is another side to this story. Some people do the opposite of coasting. They give everything they have because they are passionate about their work. They love their calling, they believe in their mission, and they do not complain. Yet passion often makes them the easiest to take advantage of.

Think about teachers who work long hours shaping young lives, then drive for ride-share companies at night just to pay bills.

Think about police officers who face death or injury from the moment they start their shift until the time they clock out. Yet, after those hours, many take on extra jobs before and after work, not to chase wealth but simply to provide a decent quality of life for their family. The sacrifice is not only physical but also the relentless demand of a profession that takes everything and then asks for more.

These are not people chasing titles. These are people who would do the work because they care, even if the money is not there. They are the ones most underpaid, undervalued, and stretched to the breaking point.

The tragedy is that while some show up and refuse to work, others show up, give everything, and still cannot survive on what they earn. Leadership cannot ignore either truth.

THE LEADERSHIP COST

Leaders who allow disengagement create two heavy costs.

- **LOST CREDIBILITY:** Teams lose faith in leaders who do not confront the obvious.
- **LOST PEOPLE:** The best workers leave, while the worst ones stay.

The sad truth is that many leaders look the other way because confrontation is uncomfortable. But silence is costly. The price of avoiding hard conversations is always paid by the whole team.

THE RESPONSE LEADERS MUST TAKE

Strong leaders cannot ignore people who show up without working. They must:

1. Set clear expectations from the start. Make the job requirements plain and non-negotiable.
2. Give people a clear vision so they understand where the organization is going and why their role matters.
3. Address bad behavior quickly before it affects the team.
4. Coach for fit if the person truly wants to work but is in the wrong role.
5. Enforce accountability when people refuse to meet standards.
6. Protect the culture so good people are not dragged down by bad examples.
7. Value passion so that people who give their all are not ignored, underpaid, or taken for granted.

Leadership is not just about inspiring. It is also about confronting. Inspiration without clarity is empty. This is high-expectation leadership. The trait of excellence sets a standard that lifts the entire organization.

WATCH OUT

Do not confuse time served with value added.

PLAIN INSIGHT

Attendance without contribution is a quiet exit in plain sight.

CASE STUDY: LEARNING TO BREATHE

A veteran clocked in and coasted. A new leader built a clear plan with measures and weekly check ins. The spark returned or the seat opened. The team got its oxygen back.

TOOL: CONTRIBUTION TRACKER

Write one concrete result you delivered this week that someone else could feel.

DRILL: START A MEETING

Pick one meeting where you usually watch. Bring one idea and one offer to help.

REFLECTION QUESTIONS

1. Where am I standing still while the mission moves?
2. What result can I deliver this week that matters to others?

3. Who will notice the difference I make today?

MODERN CONNECTION

Status lights show green while work stands still. Leaders look past the light to the output.

LEADERSHIP BRIDGE

I choose to be useful, not just present. My work will speak for me.

THE CLOSING CHALLENGE

Look at your team. Who is present but not performing? Who is holding a seat, collecting a paycheck, but not honoring the responsibility they agreed to carry? And just as importantly, who is giving everything they have and still being overlooked or underpaid?

Great leadership is not just about helping good people grow. It is also about addressing those who refuse to contribute, while protecting those who give their best from being taken for granted.

The silent exodus costs us people who walk away. The silent burden costs us people who stay but do not work. The hidden cost of passion drains the very people who hold teams together. And the clear vision gap leaves too many wandering without direction.

All four are leadership failures, and all four demand the courage to act.

CHAPTER 30:
RETIRED ON DUTY

THE COST OF LEADERSHIP is steep. It demands time, peace, and pieces of yourself. The weight is heavy, yet the change it produces makes the sacrifice worthwhile. I have lost friends, faced betrayal, carried burdens, and stood alone. I have also seen transformation rise where it once seemed impossible. Leadership is both sacrifice and a gift.

The most dangerous threat to leadership is not failure or criticism. The true danger is staying in place after passion has died. An empty seat is obvious. A filled seat without spirit is invisible poison.

Retired-on-duty leaders are everywhere. They attend meetings, send emails, and collect paychecks. Their presence looks complete, yet their hearts left long ago. They do just enough to remain. Their fire and spark have gone out, that once inspired others.

This is the illusion of presence. It resembles leadership, but it is not. It is a hollow version of what once was. These leaders stop creating, stop risking, and stop caring. They cling to old victories as if yesterday can carry today, but leadership is only present in the present moments in time.

Why do they remain? Some stay because comfort feels safe. Others stay because fear whispers that without the job they are nothing. Some stay for money, cashing their checks while shutting down emotionally. Others stay out of entitlement, convinced that seniority is a license to give less.

The cost of retiring on duty is devastating. Morale suffers when younger employees watch someone do the bare minimum and still receive reward. Opportunities are blocked because seats are filled by people who no longer grow. Culture erodes. Standards slip. Excellence fades. Mediocrity has become normal.

One retired-on-duty leader communicates a destructive message to the entire organization. That message is simple: you can stop adding value and still expect recognition. Nothing corrodes trust and excellence faster.

Leaders cannot afford to retire on duty. Too many people depend on the fire inside you. If your passion is gone, you should self-reflect. Renew your purpose or release the seat for someone ready to rise. That decision is not weakness. It is integrity. The measure of leadership is not how long a person holds a title, rather the quality of service offered during the time in the role. When passion is gone, staying becomes selfish. Stepping aside becomes leadership. Choose carefully. If you stay, stay with fire. If you cannot, leave with dignity. The world does not need more leaders in name. It needs leaders whose eyes still carry light.

THE LEADERSHIP RESPONSE

1. **IDENTIFY IT QUICKLY:** Do not confuse presence with performance. Look beyond attendance and titles to see who is truly engaged.
2. **CONFRONT IT DIRECTLY:** Honest conversations must happen. Leaders cannot allow free rides at the expense of the mission.
3. **OFFER A CHOICE:** Either rediscover your fire and re-engage, or step aside with dignity so someone else can lead with passion.
4. **PROTECT THE CULTURE:** Make it clear that no one has the right to retire on duty.

LEADERSHIP INSIGHT

A seat filled by someone retired on duty is worse than an empty seat. An empty seat can be filled with new life. A retired-on-duty seat blocks the future while draining the present.

WATCH OUT

Do not mistake a uniform for a contribution.

PLAIN INSIGHT

Excellence is not automatic. It is a daily decision.

CASE STUDY: GAINING MOMENTUM

A senior officer stayed on the schedule but off the mission. Coaching and clear standards gave him a choice. Reengage or release the seat. Either way the team regained momentum, and the public felt the difference.

TOOL: THIRTY DAY RESET

Write three specific outcomes for this month. Share them with a partner who will ask you about them every Friday.

DRILL: MAKING THE TEAM SAFE

End each shift by answering this question in writing. What did I do today that made the community safer or the team stronger?

REFLECTION QUESTIONS

1. What would my absence reveal about the value I truly added?

2. Is my presence fueling the mission or simply filling a role?
3. Do my people see me as an example to follow or a warning to avoid?
4. Who on my team has quietly retired on duty, and what am I doing about it?
5. Would I follow me if I were in their shoes?

MODERN CONNECTION

Quiet coasting spreads like a cold. Leaders stop it at the source and model the cure.

LEADERSHIP BRIDGE
I will serve like it is day one until it is my last day.

CLOSING THOUGHT

Retirement is honorable when it is chosen at the right time. Retiring while still on the clock, still in the chair, and still taking the check is different. That is betrayal, to the mission, to the culture, and to the people who are carrying the real weight. Leaders must never allow it, and true professionals must never choose it.

The future is waiting for leaders who refuse to retire on duty. Communities, schools, businesses, and families need leaders who show up with fire, courage, and heart. The mission does not need empty seats. It needs people who are alive, engaged, and willing to give their best. That is the call of leadership. That is the gift we leave behind. If you choose to stay alive in your mission, you will not just fill a chair. You will shape a legacy.

CHAPTER 31:
THE HIDDEN COST OF ABSENCE

THERE ARE PEOPLE who take pride in serving, and there are people who take pride in finding ways not to. The patterns are not hard to see. Mondays and Fridays. The day before a holiday. The day after a holiday. The long weekends that turn into longer vacations. The same names keep showing up. The same excuses keep being repeated. Sick. Injured. Family emergency. Personal issue.

Time off is not the problem. Everyone needs rest. Everyone needs recovery. Everyone needs personal time. Burnout is real, and no leader should ever want their people to collapse under the weight of the mission. The abuse of absence is different. It is when someone is not truly sick but tells the story anyway. It is when someone calls off, not because they cannot work, but because they do not want to. It is when someone brags to friends and family about how they got over on the organization. That is not rest. That is betrayal.

What they do not see is the truth. Their absence does not just fall on a supervisor. It falls on the people who showed up. The teacher covering an extra class. The nurse forced into overtime. The officer left short on a call. The worker holding the line alone. The people who were promised service feel the weight most of all.

There is another kind of absence that costs just as much. Time theft. It is the appointment that stretches into half a day gone. It is the lunch break that turns into an afternoon missing. It is the employee who says they are working from home but spends the hours doing everything but the work. Time theft is not harmless. It is a silent betrayal of both the mission and the team.

The most dangerous form of absence is not physical. It is the absence of care. Some people simply stop caring about the work, the mission, or the people they once agreed to serve. They convince themselves that the job is worthless, the supervisors are not worth following, or that their own comfort is all that matters. That mindset poisons a culture faster than any excuse. If someone no longer wants to be part of the work, then leaving may be the most honest decision they can make. Staying only to collect a paycheck while draining the team is more destructive than walking away.

Convenient absences and time theft break trust. They turn dedication into resentment. They weaken the culture and leave scars that do not heal quickly. The bragging makes it worse. To celebrate skipping the very duty you signed up for is to admit that you value comfort over calling.

LEADERSHIP LENS

Accountable leadership demands clarity here. Leaders must be strong enough to call out abuse and wise enough to protect those who truly need time away. The trait is responsibility. The standard is simple. Use your leave honestly. Take rest when you need it. Take care of your health. Do not lie. Do not scheme. Do not brag about avoiding the very people you were trusted to serve.

WATCH OUT

Do not excuse patterns of absence as harmless. Small abuses multiply into deep fractures of trust.

PLAIN INSIGHT

Absence is more than missing time. It shifts the weight onto others and erodes the culture of service.

CASE STUDY: THE PATTERN REVEALED

A school district noticed the same three teachers calling out sick every Monday for six consecutive weeks. When HR reviewed the pattern, they discovered social media posts showing weekend trips that extended into Mondays. The principal held private conversations with each teacher, presenting the attendance records and the pattern. One teacher admitted burnout and requested a mental health leave, which was granted with full support. The second teacher acknowledged the abuse and committed to change. The third teacher became defensive and resigned. The remaining staff saw that leadership protected genuine need while confronting dishonesty. Morale improved because people knew the system was fair.

TOOL: ABSENCE AUDIT

Track one week of attendance. Mark planned, genuine, and questionable call-offs. Discuss the patterns and adjust policies or coaching where needed.

DRILL: FILLING IN

Leaders fill in for one absent role for a day. Record what you learned about the burden absence creates, then share it with your team.

REFLECTION QUESTIONS

1. Who carries the weight when someone calls off?
2. How often do I excuse questionable absences instead of addressing them?
3. What message do I send when I ignore time theft?
4. Does my team know I will protect real rest and confront abuse?
5. If I disappeared tomorrow, would my absence weaken or strengthen the mission?

MODERN CONNECTION

Remote work makes time theft easier to hide. Cameras and keystrokes cannot replace culture. Integrity is still the measure.

LEADERSHIP BRIDGE
I will honor true rest, confront false absence, and protect the weight my people carry.

CONCLUSION
CROSSING THE BRIDGE

LEADERSHIP HAS BEEN the journey of my life. From a young boy living in the inner city making decisions that could have cost me everything to standing in the role of Chief of Police, I have learned that leadership is not about titles, uniforms, or positions. It is about choices, responsibility, and the courage to keep moving forward even when the cost is high.

This book is about real leadership rather than perfect leadership. The kind that makes mistakes and learns from them. The kind that sacrifices, too much at times. The kind that can build trust and lose it. The kind that has the power to change lives, organizations, and communities when handled with integrity.

I have shared stories of the good, the bad, and the ugly. I have been honest about the costs, both public and personal. I have shown the weight of accountability, the challenge of balancing family, and the loneliness that often comes with carrying responsibility. I have also shown the promise that comes with perseverance, trust, and transformation.

The truth is that leadership belongs to all of us. You do not need a badge or a title to lead. Leadership is in the choices you make when no one is watching. It is in the way you treat people who cannot offer you anything in return. It is in the blueprint you cast for your life, your family, your organization, or your community.

I want you to understand that leadership will often cost you something. It will challenge you, test you, and demand sacrifices. If you are willing to endure with integrity, courage, and humility, the reward is far greater than the sacrifice. The reward is the power to bring change.

We are living in a time when the world is desperate for leaders who are real. Not perfect. Not polished. But real. Leaders who admit mistakes, who value people over power, and who use their influence to lift others higher. The world does not need more bosses. It needs more bridge builders.

My challenge to you is simple: build your bridge. Build it with trust. Build it with accountability. Build it with courage. Build it with purpose. Do not just build it for yourself. Build it for those who will walk with you. Those who will follow your example, and those who need to know that leadership can still be honorable.

SHIFT: The Cost of Leadership, The Power of Change

I thank the Creator for guiding my steps and giving me the strength to keep going when the weight felt unbearable. I thank you for taking this journey with me through these pages.

Now it is your turn. The cost is real, but so is the promise. The question is not whether leadership will require something from you. The question is: are you willing to endure so that others can experience the power of change?

When your time is done, may people say they were better because you were there. That is the cost of leadership. That is the power of change. That is the bridge worth building.

LEADERSHIP SNAPSHOT

These are only a few leadership styles and traits out of many. They are presented here to give you a quick glance at how leaders often show up and what qualities matter most. Use this page as a mirror to reflect on who you are as a leader.

LEADERSHIP STYLES (AS I SEE THEM)

- **VISIONARY LEADER** – Sees beyond the present and paints a picture of the future that people want to follow.

- **SERVANT LEADER** – Puts people first, lifting others up and building the team before chasing results.
- **TRANSFORMATIONAL LEADER** – Challenges the old way of doing things and inspires change that reshapes culture.
- **TRANSACTIONAL LEADER** – Leads through structure, clear rules, and accountability. Rewards and consequences guide the team.
- **CHARISMATIC LEADER** – Wins people with energy, presence, and the ability to inspire in the moment.
- **AUTOCRATIC LEADER** – Makes firm decisions with little outside input. Provides clarity, control, and direction.
- **DEMOCRATIC LEADER** – Values input and collaboration, giving people a voice in the process and decisions.
- **LAISSEZ-FAIRE LEADER** – Steps back and gives freedom, trusting people to lead themselves and solve problems.

LEADERSHIP TRAITS (A FEW THAT MATTER TO ME)

- **INTEGRITY** – Doing the right thing even when nobody is watching.
- **RESILIENCE** – Taking the hit, standing back up, and moving forward.
- **DECISIVENESS** – Making the tough calls when others freeze.
- **EMPATHY** – Listening with compassion, not just with the ears.

- **VISION** – Seeing beyond today and helping others see it too.
- **ADAPTABILITY** – Adjusting when the ground shifts instead of breaking down.
- **ACCOUNTABILITY** – Owning mistakes as quickly as successes.
- **COURAGE** – Speaking truth, standing firm, and facing fear head-on.
- **HUMILITY** – Staying grounded no matter how high you rise.
- **CONSISTENCY** – Leading steady so people know they can trust the path.

Great leadership is always simple to explain but difficult to live. Humility, integrity, courage, and vision are not complicated traits, but they require daily discipline. Leaders who commit to them change not only their teams but also their communities.

AUTHOR'S NOTE

If you have made it this far, thank you. Not just for reading, but for walking across this bridge with me. Writing this book forced me to look back at victories, mistakes, pride, and pain. Leadership is not a straight road. It is full of turns and lessons that stay with you.

I did not write this for applause. I wrote it because someone needed these words. Maybe an officer searching for meaning in the badge. Maybe a CEO wondering if the sacrifices are worth it. Maybe a parent torn between work and children. Whoever you are, I hope my story gives you courage to lead with integrity, humility, and purpose.

I am still a work in progress. I do not have all the answers. I do believe that one of life's greatest gifts is to create value for someone else. That is the essence of leadership. That is what gives sacrifice meaning.

As I step into the next chapter of my life, beyond the badge and into new opportunities to teach, speak, and serve, I will carry the lessons and bridges this journey gave me. My hope is that you will take these lessons, apply them in your own way, and build bridges of your own.

Thank you for trusting me with your time. Thank you for listening to my story.

SHIFT: The Cost of Leadership, The Power of Change

Thank you for choosing to lead in a world that needs true leaders.

— **CURTIS ADAMS**

CALL TO ACTION

Thank you for reading *SHIFT: The Cost of Leadership, The Power of Change*. If these pages challenged you or opened your perspective, the next step is action.

LET US STAY CONNECTED: •

🌐 Website: www.curtisad.com

✉ Email: curtisad777@gmail.com •

🔗 LinkedIn: linkedin.com/in/curtis-adams-51275754

📘 Facebook: facebook.com/share/1Fq3PdndxR •

📷 Instagram: instagram.com/bcsdchiefadams

🎥 YouTube: @curtisadams

Whether you are leading in a school, a department, a business, a church, or at home, I believe the lessons in this book can be used to build bridges, restore trust, and transform culture.

If this book added value, share it with someone who needs it. Start a discussion group with your team. Your leadership journey does not end here. It begins again with each decision you make from this day forward.

Together we can build leaders who heal, build, and leave people better than they found them.

ENDNOTES

ROSA PARKS – Rosa Parks' decision to keep her seat on a Montgomery bus in 1955 sparked the Montgomery Bus Boycott. Brinkley, D. (2000). *Rosa Parks: A Life*. Viking.

HARRIET TUBMAN – Larson, K. C. (2004). *Bound for the Promised Land: Harriet Tubman, Portrait of an American Hero*. One World.

JACKIE ROBINSON – Broke Major League Baseball's color barrier in 1947, facing intense hostility but choosing dignity over retaliation. Robinson, J., & Duckett, A. (1995). *I Never Had It Made: An Autobiography of Jackie Robinson*. Harper Perennial.

SATYA NADELLA AT MICROSOFT – Nadella, S. (2017). *Hit Refresh: The Quest to Rediscover Microsoft's Soul and Imagine a Better Future for Everyone*. Harper Business.

ABRAHAM LINCOLN – Quoted as saying, 'Nearly all men can stand adversity, but if you want to test a man's character, give him power.' Basler, R. P. (Ed.). (1953). *The Collected Works of Abraham Lincoln*. Rutgers University Press.

HOWARD SCHULTZ – Returned to Starbucks in 2008, rebuilding the company by listening to employees and focusing on culture. Schultz, H., & Yang, J. (2011). *Onward: How*

Starbucks Fought for Its Life without Losing Its Soul. Rodale Books.

WINSTON CHURCHILL – Inspired Britain with speeches during World War II, such as 'We shall fight on the beaches.' Gilbert, M. (1991). *Winston S. Churchill: Finest Hour 1939-1941*. Houghton Mifflin.

INDRA NOOYI – Former CEO of PepsiCo, who shared her struggles of balancing leadership and family. Nooyi, I., & Govindarajan, R. (2021). *My Life in Full: Work, Family, and Our Future*. Portfolio.

GEORGE WASHINGTON – After leading the Continental Army, he stepped down from power voluntarily, modeling servant leadership. Ellis, J. J. (2005). *His Excellency: George Washington*. Vintage.

JIM COLLINS – Identified 'Level 5 Leaders' in his book. Collins, J. (2001). *Good to Great: Why Some Companies Make the Leap... and Others Do Not*. Harper Business.

DWIGHT D. EISENHOWER – Delegated authority during World War II, trusting his commanders to act independently. Ambrose, S. E. (1995). *D-Day, June 6, 1944: The Climactic Battle of World War II*. Simon & Schuster.

REED HASTINGS – Hastings, R., & Meyer, E. (2020). *No Rules: Netflix and the Culture of Reinvention*. Penguin Press.

STEVE JOBS – Built Apple's culture of innovation that endured beyond his leadership. Isaacson, W. (2011). *Steve Jobs*. Simon & Schuster.

THEODORE ROOSEVELT – As New York City Police Commissioner, personally patrolled precincts to enforce accountability. Brands, H. W. (1997). *T.R.: The Last Romantic*. Basic Books.

JOHNSON & JOHNSON – The 1982 Tylenol recall set a new corporate standard for crisis management. Fearn-Banks, K. (2016). *Crisis Communications: A Casebook Approach*. Routledge.

WATERGATE SCANDAL – A culture of cover-ups destroyed public trust in the presidency. Bernstein, C., & Woodward, B. (1974). *All the President's Men*. Simon & Schuster.

ANNE MULCAHY – Mulcahy, A. (2009). "Saving Xerox: Lessons in Leadership." *Harvard Business Review*.

ENRON – Its collapse became a textbook case of corporate fraud. McLean, B., & Elkind, P. (2004). *The Smartest Guys in the Room: The Amazing Rise and Scandalous Fall of Enron*. Portfolio.

MARTIN LUTHER KING JR. – Martin Luther King Jr.'s leadership during the Civil Rights Movement embodied courage, vision, and the power of nonviolent change. King, M. L., Jr. (1963). *Strength to Love*. Harper & Row.

ALAN MULALLY – As CEO of Ford, Alan Mulally turned the company around during the 2008 financial crisis through transparency, teamwork, and relentless focus on "One Ford." Taylor, A. (2013). *American Icon: Alan Mulally and the Fight to Save Ford Motor Company*. Crown Business.

WALT DISNEY – Walt Disney transformed imagination into reality, building a global brand by dreaming bigger than his time. Thomas, B. (1994). *Walt Disney: An American Original*. Disney Editions.

JOHN C. MAXWELL – Leadership expert John Maxwell has written extensively on influence, growth, and developing others, defining leadership as "influence—nothing more, nothing less." Maxwell, J. C. (1998). *The 21 Irrefutable Laws of Leadership: Follow Them and People Will Follow You*. Thomas Nelson.

PETER DRUCKER – Peter Drucker's phrase 'Culture eats strategy for breakfast' is from *Management Challenges for the 21st Century* (Harper Business, 1999).

AUTHOR: CHIEF CURTIS ADAMS

CURTIS ADAMS is the Chief of Police for the Bibb County School District in Macon, Georgia. Shaped by resilience, he rose from the inner-city streets of Chicago to become a voice for change in policing and leadership.

Before becoming Chief, Curtis served as Major for the Atlanta Public Schools Police Department, where he helped shape school safety and leadership development. He previously worked at the Sheriff's Office in Florida as a deputy and instructor, and with the Atlanta Police Department as both an officer and an academy instructor. Earlier in his career, he served as a juvenile probation officer, a mental health worker, and a football and wrestling coach. Each stage of his journey added lessons in trust, accountability, and perseverance that continue to guide his leadership today.

Curtis is the author of *Building Bridges: A Chief's Quest for Change in Policing*, *7 Bridges: A Father's Reckoning*, the children's book *Chief Adams' Bridge of Kindness*, and *Bridge of Kindness Coloring & Activity Book*. His writing combines personal storytelling, leadership insights, and lessons about service, sacrifice, and resilience.

He has spoken to audiences nationwide, including law enforcement agencies, schools, churches, leadership conferences, businesses, and corporations. His message of integrity, accountability, and compassion resonates with leaders across all fields.

Curtis lives by his motto: "One of life's greatest gifts is creating value for someone else other than yourself." He invites readers to explore his other books to continue the message of healing, truth, and service.

Books - Curtis Adams

curtisad.com

SHIFT: The Cost of Leadership, The Power of Change